GENDER ISSUES IN FIELD RESEARCH

CAROL A. B. WARREN
University of Southern California

Qualitative Research Methods,
Volume 9

SAGE PUBLICATIONS
The Publishers of Professional Social Science
Newbury Park   Beverly Hills   London   New Delhi

Copyright © 1988 by Sage Publications, Inc.

For information address:

SAGE Publications, Inc.
2111 West Hillcrest Drive
Newbury Park, California 91320

SAGE Publications Inc.
275 South Beverly Drive
Beverly Hills
California 90212

SAGE Publications Ltd.
28 Banner Street
London EC1Y 8QE
England

SAGE PUBLICATIONS India Pvt. Ltd.
M-32 Market
Greater Kailash I
New Delhi 110 048 India

Printed in the United States of America

Library of Congress Cataloging-in-Publication Data

Main entry under title:

Warren, Carol A. B., 1944-
    Gender issues in field research / by Carol A. B. Warren.
      p. cm. -- (Qualitative research methods ; v. 9)
    Bibliography: p.
    ISBN 0-8039-3098-4 (pbk.) : v. 9 ISBN 0-8039-3097-6 :
    1. Social sciences--Field work. 2. Anthropology--Field work.
3. Sociology--Field work. 4. Sex differences. I. Title.
II. Series.
H62.W283   1988   87-22450
300'.72--dc19   CIP

CONTENTS

To Barbara, with love

EDITORS' INTRODUCTION

Fieldworkers would like to believe that whatever they see, hear, and write up as a result of their research experience in a particular setting is what any other similarly trained and situated fieldworker would also see, hear, and write up. This is the ethnographic conceit and, to a certain extent, it has kept the enterprise going for the past fifty or so years. Such a conceit has had its day, however. Increasingly, fieldwork is regarded as a highly and almost hauntingly personal method for which no programmatic guides can be written.

Carol A. B. Warren takes up these issues in Volume 9 of the Sage Qualitative Research Methods Series by focusing on the role gender plays in field research. In essence, Warren shows that ethnography, as the polished product of field research, cannot be understood by the writer or the reader without explicitly taking account of the ways the gender of the researcher influences both fieldwork relations and the production of the final report. Since gender is a key organizing device in all cultures, male and female researchers will always be treated differently by those they study and thus they will come to know different aspects of the cultures they investigate.

Gender Issues in Field Research draws upon both anthropological and sociological examples to make its points. Crucial to the monograph are the various ways particular researchers have attempted to manage and, in some cases, modify the opportunities and constraints posed by gender. The lessons here are idiosyncratic but no less important as a result. Certainly they point to the fact that gender matters in virtually all aspects of social research.

How it matters is of course the crucial question facing fieldworkers. It is a question that can be addressed usefully from many perspectives and several particularly promising ones are suggested in the book. But, reader beware. This is not a book about how to minimize the role gender plays in field research. It is first and foremost a book about how gender operates in the field. The idea is not to deny gender a place in research but to examine the role it plays as a topic itself deserving of research

5

interest. And, as Carol Warren makes clear, there is much for us to learn.

John Van Maanen
Peter K. Manning
Marc L. Miller

PREFACE

The purpose of this small volume is to summarize the "state of the art" of gender issues in fieldwork, in both anthropology and sociology.[1] Gender is a focal, an organizing category in social life and social science. What this means for field researchers is that we must develop a sensitivity to issues of gender both when we do our fieldwork, and when we write it up. Since our methodology has as its central commitment the unity of the interpretive process—of the biography and history of the setting and the biography and history of the researcher—then it is vital to understand the place of gender in social research.

What is that place? Over the past decade or so, social scientists have become increasingly concerned with the reflexive nature of fieldwork methods. The myth of the ethnographer as any person, without gender, personality or historical location, who would objectively (at the very least intersubjectively) produce the same findings as any other person has been increasingly challenged. This volume draws together one aspect of this epistemological challenge to the myth of any person: the impact of gender on fieldwork relationships and the production of ethnography. It is based on both sociological and anthropological sources (including my own fieldwork experiences), although relatively more on the anthropological. There has been much more concern for gender issues in anthropological than in sociological fieldwork. And this concern has a longer history. While anthropologists were writing methodologically about gender as early as the 1920s and 1930s, sociologists did not begin to analyze it systematically until the mid-1970s.[2]

I want to state several limitations of this analysis at the outset. First, gender is only one of many personal characteristics that shape the course of fieldwork; age, social class, and race or ethnicity are other obvious influences.[3] So my focus is on gender rather than on the totality of characteristics that assume significance in the fieldwork process. Second, I deal only tangentially with the issue of gender in intensive interviewing. Third, there is considerably more about women than men in my discussion, which reflects the emphasis on women in the methodological literature. I suspect that this methodological "feminocentrism" (which contrasts with the "androcentrism" of substantive and theoretical concerns) arises from the paradoxical situation of women field researchers. From the moment of their entrance into fieldwork in anthropology and sociology in the early twentieth century, women scholars did their research against the background of taken-for-granted androcentric assumptions about social life. Over time, these assumptions became the object of inquiry, resulting in a self-consciousness about issues related to women in the field.

Finally, the historical and cross-cultural specification of the generalizations I present is less developed than I would have liked. Although I use cross-cultural materials from anthropological ethnography, I provide only a limited sense of the embeddedness of gender themes in the rich details of different cultures. Similarly, although I attend to historical differences in fieldwork accounts from the 1920s to the 1980s, this theme is not as elaborated as full contextualization would warrant.

Historical location also affects, reflexively, the ways in which gender issues in field research are thought about and written about. As Hunt (1984) notes, although the literature on gender issues in fieldwork has been developed only over the past decade, its epistemological assumptions have changed during that time. She adds that the "major [older] studies . . . do not see gender as negotiable," criticizing my work with Rasmussen in the 1970s because we

> suggest that gender is an attribute that affects rapport and defines the quality and type of data gathered precisely because it is on the order of a deep category that resists negotiation. It follows that, as the fieldworker remains encapsulated in the stereotypical role designated by subjects, women researchers are likely to have limited access to data in masculine settings. The practical consequence is that these authors blatantly justified the exclusion of female observers . . . from a team study of police because the police view women as sex objects and were committed to protecting them from seeing routine policework. (Hunt, 1984, p. 286)

The 1980s, however, have seen the development of a perspective that frames gender not as an ascribed role but as a "negotiated" one, based on both the gender features of the setting and the interactions of fieldworker and respondents over time (Hunt, 1984; Lederman, 1986; Turnbull, 1986).

My own fieldwork biography is located in a history (both substantive and disciplinary) that spans the late 1960s to mid-1970s.[4] This socio-historical location has shaped my view of gender and other roles as assigned to the fieldworker by the "natives," with the negotiation of rapport taking place within that context, rather than the other way around (Hunt, 1984). Unlike Hunt (1984) I tend to see gender not as an object of fieldwork negotiation, but as part of the structural grounds upon which negotiation takes place.

This discussion of gender and women in the field is divided into four parts. First, I indicate the ways in which gender shapes social life and social science. Next, I look at the process of doing fieldwork: entree and access to settings by gender; gender and research relations in the field, and gender and "women's place." I then examine some of the ways in which data analysis and the development of knowledge in social science has been influenced by feminist theory and by a discourse analysis sensitive to gender. The final section, "Warnings and Advice" is intended to give some indication to the novice fieldworker of how to integrate these understandings about gender, field relations, and knowledge into the everyday practice of ethnography.[5]

GENDER ISSUES IN FIELD RESEARCH

CAROL A. B. WARREN
University of Southern California

1. GENDER IN SOCIAL LIFE AND SOCIAL SCIENCE

Being a man or woman is at the core of our social lives and of our inner selves. Gender and age (Foucault's [1980] arguments notwithstanding) are among the basic categories of the social fabric; the elaboration of them into the division of labor forms the bedrock of culture in history. Living within a society, or visiting one as a fieldworker, presupposes a gendered interaction, a gendered conversation, and a gendered interpretation. Just as all knowledge—even language itself—is political, reflecting power relations (Foucault, 1978), all knowledge is gendered.

The interconnections between knowledge, power, and gender in social life and social science have been the subject of increasingly explicit recognition, in both anthropology and sociology, by feminist scholars in particular. In anthropology, the focus of feminist scholarship has been on the rediscovery of the female heritage not only in the non-Western settings studied by anthropologists but also in the discipline itself. Thus contemporary feminist anthropologists are interested both in the careers of their predecessors, and in the non-Western "women's worlds" into which female fieldworkers have traditionally gained access. In

AUTHOR'S NOTE: Material quoted throughout this volume from Jennifer Hunt, "The Development of Rapport Through the Negotiation of Gender in Field Work Among Police," *Human Organization, 3*, 283-296 (1984), is reprinted by permission of the author.

sociology, by contrast, the major methodological commitment of feminist scholarship has not been to ethnography but to historical and structural analysis, particularly of women's place in the production and reproduction of the social order. What these social science approaches have in common, however, is their contrast with the androcentric social science that preceded academic feminism; the assumption that male scholars were the paradigm of scholar, and that male worlds were the worlds—the only worlds.

Indeed, when women first went into fieldwork, in the 1920s and 1930s, scholarship was a male domain. Neither sociology nor anthropology was at that time an entirely reputable discipline; the social sciences in what is now seen as their classic era attracted marginal people, including women (Kuper, 1973). Both in Britain and in the United States during the 1920s there were approximately equal numbers of male and female anthropology graduate students, despite the many barriers to women's full acceptance in any discipline:

> It is tempting to attribute the receptivity of anthropology to women to the nature of the subject matter and its practitioners, individuals who were inherently interested in marginal groups and minorities. But the "feminization" of an academic field was characteristic of disciplines with slow growth rates and a general lack of employment prospects. . . . As with other fields of science, although women might enter anthropology in almost equal numbers to men, they were less likely to get jobs in academic departments, especially in co-educational universities. (Lutkehaus, forthcoming, a)

The situation in the Chicago School during the 1920s and 1930s was similar. Although sociology had relatively greater prestige in the United States than anthropology did in Britain, it still remained in the shadow of the "real sciences" on the one hand, and the "real letters" on the other. And although there were case study and interview dissertations written by women graduate students during the Chicago heyday, almost all those studies that survived as classics were written by men (The Jack Roller, The Gold Coast and the Slum) and almost all those graduate students who survived as professors were men (exceptions on both counts include Helen Hughes and Sylvia Clavan).

Unfortunately, the history of women graduate students in the Chicago School has yet to be written; we have few glimpses either of their professional situation or of the contingencies of their research.[6] But the history of women in British anthropology in the same era affords us some glimpses of early definitions of women's "special problems" in the field. Lutkehaus (forthcoming, a) describes the prevailing concern for women's protection:

> In 1932 Camilla Wedgwood received a fellowship from the Australian National Research Council to carry out fieldwork in Melanesia on culture contact . . . [her male European colleagues] in New Guinea did not welcome the idea of a single woman coming out to do fieldwork on her own. This was a period in the history of New Guinea in which the fear among whites of sexual assault to females was at its height . . . with little concrete evidence that white women were actually in danger of sexual assault. But [a male colleague of Wedgwood's wrote to another male anthropologist that] "if any more lady anthropologists are thinking of coming out here you had better suggest that they bring a husband with them. I know of no place where a woman can work without fear of molestation from the natives."

Contemporary fieldwork concerns have a different focus than women's safety from rape and molestation. The development of an epistemology of fieldwork has made both women and men more attentive to the reflexive influence of the personal characteristics of the fieldworker, the methods and purposes of the study, and the setting's characteristics. Entree to the field, access to the different worlds that exist within worlds, relations with key informants and others, and the way in which feelings and ideas shape communications about the field experience have been the focus of increasing methodological concern within the social sciences.

2. GENDER AND
FIELDWORK RELATIONSHIPS

There is a vast and growing literature on gender and fieldwork relationships, eclipsing scholarly interest in other personal characteristics such as ethnicity or age (perhaps because there are relatively more women fieldworkers than either minority or elderly ones). This literature can be read—and I will in this section so read it—as a reflection of interactions that occurred between gendered fieldworkers in different times and places. The literature can also be read—and I will do so in the next section—as text; as a set of fieldwork myths, shaped by various disciplinary and rhetorical requirements.

For the first, and more conventional purpose, it is useful to distinguish several themes in the gender-fieldwork literature, themes that are generally framed in a discussion of rapport and trust in fieldwork relationships.[7] These are entree, finding a place within the culture, sexuality and the body, and sexual politics. Much of the discussion of these themes takes the form of anecdotes, without consideration of how the interactions described shaped the analysis. Furthermore, this set of themes, and the focus on gender itself, reflect issues cogent to Western culture, which tends (for example) toward a preoccupation with sex and with physical appearance, and issues cogent to Western academia, which has been embroiled over the past two decades in controversies over sexism and sexual politics.

Entree and the Web of Gender

The fieldworker's initial reception by the host society is a reflection of cultural contextualization of the fieldworker's characteristics, which include marital status, age, physical appearance, presence and number of children, and ethnic, racial, class, or national differences as well as gender.[8] Gender in our own society refers to the ways in which biological sex roles are culturally elaborated: to the values, beliefs, technologies, and general fates to which we assign women and men. Other cultures do not separate cultural from biological roles in this way; the view of biology as destiny is far more ancient and pervasive than our own ideology would permit. Nor do other cultures make the distinctions we do between sexual identity, gender identity, and sexual behavior; categories such as gayness, lesbianism, transsexualism, and transvestism are historically and culturally determined. On the other hand, the social institutions of marriage and family have a more pervasive cultural warrant. The fieldworker's marital status is of particular significance to anthropological informants, since most "primitive" cultures take kinship bonds as the fundamental source of social structure and social order. As Angrosino (1986, p. 68) comments, a "single person is a rarity in most societies where anthropologists have done fieldwork." While male anthropologists have reported fewer practical research problems with their unmarried status than women, they indicate the near-universality of the expectation that adult males should be sexually active (Angrosino, 1986; Whitehead, 1986, and see below). But an unmarried, childless adult woman has no fully legitimate social place in most cultures unless, perhaps, she is elderly and thus androgynized (Golde, 1986). As Peggy

Golde (1986, p. 80) said of her entree into the culture of the Nahua Indians of Mexico:

> What was problematic was that I was unmarried and older than was reasonable for an unmarried girl to be, I was without the protection of my family, and I traveled alone, as an unmarried, virginal girl would never do. They found it hard to understand how I, so obviously attractive in their eyes, could still be single. . . . Being an unmarried girl meant that I should not drink, smoke, go about alone at night, visit during the day without a real errand, speak of such topics as sex or pregnancy, entertain boys or men in my house except in the presence of older people, or ask too many questions of any kind.

Married women anthropologists fit some cultural expectations while violating others, often those concerned with gender dominance. Ernestine Friedl (1986, p. 198), describing her fieldwork in a Greek village accompanied by her husband, commented:

> At the outset . . . I was involved in a formally and publicly wife-dominated enterprise in a society that was husband-centered to a degree even greater than is customary in Western Europe and America. Half deliberately and half as a matter of natural development we pragmatically compensated for this anomaly. My husband became the spokesman for the two of us in Athens and the village.

Where the working partner in a marital team is a woman anthropologist and her husband is not working, he may be able and willing to assume the main burden of household chores; indeed, an equalization of household labor seems to have become increasingly common among academics between the 1960s and 1980s (compare, for example, Freedman [1986] with Oboler [1986]). But this etic adaptation can conflict with local cultural norms concerning the proper sphere of women's and men's work. During her fieldwork in Rumania, Diane Freedman (1986, pp. 344-345) noted that

> while the villagers knew that our own household customs differed from theirs, we were expected to conform somewhat to ideal patterns of the sexual division of labor. In this pattern, household and garden tasks are the domain of the women, and heavy agricultural work and the care of large animals are left to the men. . . . Our household was different since Robert had neither land to till nor animals to tend. As a result, he did

more than half of our housekeeping. Villagers were scandalized by our customs on this issue.... Men's reaction to our system [of drawing water from the well, done in the village by women, but in the Freedman household by Robert] were divided. Some thought it amusing, while others felt that Robert was degrading himself by doing women's work. The women, by contrast, considered it a positive sign of Robert's concern for me. Even the women, however, had limits of custom beyond which they would not be drawn. When they realized that Robert was also washing clothes, I was advised that he should do this in the house and that I should then hang the clothes outside; otherwise my reputation as a good wife would suffer.

Although a husband-wife team may be an ideal way of getting to know both male and female worlds within a culture (see below), the conduct of the spouses must remain enough within the bounds of local norms to be acceptable to informants (Mead, 1986).

The existence of children affects host reception of the anthropological couple. Carolyn Fleuhr-Lobban says of her fieldwork in the Sudan that

in a society where the extended family is the norm and the value placed on family life is high, there is no question in my mind that being identified as part of a family, originally with my husband and later with our daughter Josina, was an asset, possibly even a vital element in conducting successful field research. (Fleuhr-Lobban & Lobban, 1986, p. 188)

Being married allowed Fleuhr-Lobban access into activities reserved for married women only, such as "the relaxing pleasures of long sessions where my hands and feet were dyed with henna and various oils and perfumes were applied to my skin" (Fleuhr-Lobban & Lobban, 1986, p. 189). Having a child permitted the Lobbans more intensive and extensive access into the family-centered world of the Sudan (pp. 189-191).

Regina Oboler (1986) reports a qualitative difference in her fieldwork after she became pregnant. Although pregnancy drained her physically, making the tasks of fieldwork more difficult, it had a positive effect on field relationships. She said that as news of her pregnancy spread among her Kenyan informants,

a remarkable thing happened: my rapport with the women, which I already thought was quite good, took a sudden, dramatic turn for the better. In people's minds I had moved from the category "probably barren woman" to "childbearing woman," similar to a change of gender. . . . Men who had been urging Leon to take a second wife no longer did so. (Oboler, 1986, p. 45)

In the context of the web of gender, age, and children, women anthropologists from the 1920s to the present time have found their research focused on "women's issues" and women's settings, mainly the domestic sphere, child rearing, health, and nutrition. In part, this has resulted from expectations associated with their home territory—with Western anthropologists' cultural assumptions. But in addition, the societies studied by anthropologists are often highly gender-segregated, with numerous roles and activities taken by one gender and banned to the other. Niara Sudarkasa (1986, p. 181), for example, notes that in her study of the Yoruba:

> I was never expected to enter into, and never did see, certain aspects of the life of men in the town. I never witnessed any ceremonies that were barred to women. Whenever I visited compounds I sat with the women while the men gathered in the parlors or in front of the compounds. . . . I never entered any of the places where men sat around to drink beer or palm wine and to chat.

The literature indicates that women anthropologists may confine their fieldwork to women's and children's worlds and not attempt entree into men's settings, or they may seek acceptance by men as well as women. Margaret Mead (1986) claims that the conduct of women anthropologists in the field is influenced by the degree of her adoption of the traditional-female role within her own culture. She argues that there are two styles of woman anthropologist: the ones with "deeply feminine interests and abilities" who interest themselves, in the field, with the affairs of women and children, and the "masculinely oriented" ones bored with women and children who work alone and attempt to use male informants and study male worlds (Mead, 1986). Mead herself did fieldwork in various cultures between 1928 and 1967, as part of a husband-wife team, alone, and in collaboration with other anthropologist couples.

But women's worlds are not necessarily open to all women. Gender alone is not enough to win full acceptance into female concerns, especially those related to sexuality and reproduction. Nancie Gonzalez (1986), for example, indicates that married Guatemalan women with children consider it rude and embarrassing to discuss pregnancy or childbirth not only with unmarried women but also with childless ones. Although a youthful Dona Davis (1986) was able to converse freely with the middle-aged women of Newfoundland about sexuality and childbirth, when she asked specific interview questions about menopause she shocked and alienated her respondents (Davis, 1986, p. 256).

Similarly, maleness alone may not ensure access to all male worlds. Ernestine Friedl comments that in the Greek village she studied, the male role included a "macho willingness to boast about sex, use sexual swear words, and make sex jokes." But because her husband was a professor, and thus of a higher class, the Greek village men would not do these things in his presence, just as they would not in hers because of her gender. Friedl indicates that the couple obtained less information than they would have liked about the "attitudes, values, and general behavior of young unmarried men" (Friedl, 1986, p. 213); despite the assistance of a male collaborator, she did not have one who was also young and of the same social class as the villagers.

While women social scientists have historically sought access to male worlds, male social scientists are rarely interested in the sphere of women—which is in most cultures the world of the domestic (and therefore by modern Western definitions insignificant)—except occasionally for comparative purposes (Fleuhr-Lobban & Lobban, 1986, p. 183). An exception is black anthropologist Norris Brock Johnson's fieldwork in a midwestern U.S. elementary school (1986). He attributed the initial resistance of the female teachers to his presence to the "male hegemony" (1986, p. 167) in which female authority and territory were routinely undermined, and female sexual status took precedence over professional status:

> Male custodians had free access and routinely sauntered into the classroom unannounced, mostly while classes were in session. Many times the [male] principal would walk into the classroom, without knocking, to make an announcement, often blithely interrupting the teacher . . . the role and status of the female classroom teacher involved a gender expectation of subservience. . . . The gender expectation seemed to be that males are sexually aggressive toward females irrespective of place or situation . . . [the teachers] wanted to find out if I was "safe": that is, would I recognize their professional status and act appropriately, or would I act like a man and exhibit sexually inappropriate behavior. (Johnson, 1986, pp. 167-168)

Johnson gained acceptance from the teachers over time by not acting like (his image of their image of) a traditional male: by respecting their authority and territory, and by not flirting with them.

Sociologists—and anthropologists who, like Johnson (1986), study Western locales—also encounter closed worlds and secret societies wholly or partially delimited by gender. For example, when I did my dissertation study of a male secretive gay community during the late 1960s and early 1970s, I was able to do fieldwork in those parts of the setting dedicated to sociability and leisure—bars, parties, family gatherings. I was not, however, able to observe in those parts of the setting dedicated to sexuality—even quasi-public settings such as homosexual bath houses (see Styles, 1979) and "tearooms" (see Humphreys, 1979). Thus my portrait of the gay community is only a partial one, bounded by the social roles assigned to females within the male homosexual world (Warren, 1972).

There are other settings where initial entree is not restricted by gender, but where internal access is affected by it. The research I did in a drug rehabilitation center is an example (see Warren, 1974). This institution was open to both male and female residents. But as a female researcher, and over several months of observation, I found that men were generally much more ready to talk to me than women. Furthermore, I was generally perceived as harmless by the males, and afforded access bordering on trespass. I vividly remember one day deciding to go upstairs, an action expressly forbidden to anyone not resident in the facility. Someone started to protest; the protest was silenced by a male voice saying, "aah, what harm can she do, she's only a broad." Upstairs I went.

Research in organizations has taught me about the invisibility of the servant female in Western society. Women in organizations have traditionally been file clerks, secretaries, and, more recently, data processors and computer workers. Wandering around settings such as a psychiatric hospital and a court, and even investigating the contents of file drawers, have drawn me hardly a glance from the males engaged in more "important business." Other women fieldworkers report similar experiences of invisibility. After all, the social place of women in Western society has traditionally been to stand behind men, out of their sight: as mothers, wives, nurses, secretaries, and servants.

Finding a Place

The man or woman entering a strange culture becomes a stranger; most non-Western as well as Western cultures are today familiar with strangers. Foreign men and women who appear, and make themselves at home, in a Sudanese village, Rumanian school, or Newfoundland town are part of the landscape of contemporary life. Their place in the society (according to Hunt, 1984, their gender) is negotiated from the existing cultural stock of knowledge and action available to define and cope with strangers. The didactic methodological literature (for example, Lofland & Lofland, 1985) focuses on the problem of researcher-as-stranger role-stance: what role to adopt in a given setting, whether overt or secret, seeker or savant.

My own research experience (most recently in various medical, psychiatric, and legal organizations) has led me to conclude that role taking in fieldwork is subsumed by a more interactive process in which respondents assign the fieldworker to what they see as his or her proper place in the social order. In the mental health court I studied, for example, where young women were typically either law students or assistants or visiting nursing students, I was treated as one or another of these social types, even by people to whom I had mentioned, more than once, that I was a professor and a researcher. In the mental hospitals I visited with court personnel, despite my introduction as professor and researcher, I was taken for a visiting student, generally a nursing student (Warren, 1982). Male visitors were more often taken for attorneys, psychiatrists, or (again) law students, never nursing students or nurses. During my research in the secret gay community in the late 1960s, I found that I was often defined as a fag hag (in other locales a faggotina or fruit fly), a fairly harmless if buffoonish role. As I have detailed elsewhere, the male gay community of the late 1960s and early 1970s assigned roles to heterosexual (and to a lesser extent lesbian) women based on their participation in the sociable—certainly not the sexual—dimensions of the subculture. I was, to many, a fag hag—a woman afraid of or alienated from the world of straight men, who had found unthreatening fun and attention in the gay world (Warren, 1972).

Depending upon the culture and the fieldworker (his or her gender, social ties, and projects), roles into which the stranger is tentatively fitted can range from adoptive child to spy. And they change over time. Anthropologists, especially young unmarried women, are often assigned the role of adoptive daughter or child of the village or tribe (see Golde, 1986). Jean Briggs (1986, p. 40), describes the role of "Kapluna daughter" she was given among the Eskimo:

Categorization of me as a child was probably determined by several factors: I had introduced myself as one who wanted to "learn"... and I had asked to be adopted as a "daughter"; I was obviously ignorant of [the culture's] proprieties and skills. The fact that I am a woman may also have facilitated my categorization as a child in several respects . . . in order to be considered properly adult a woman must have children, and I had none . . . the role of an adult woman was virtually closed to me, whereas had I been a man I might have earned an adult role as a fisherman and hunter, as some [males] who have lived among Eskimos appear to have done.

Laura Nader (1986, p. 111) notes that in her study of the Shias in Lebanon she was placed in the role of "sister of men . . . a natural role that a woman anthropologist could walk into, should she wish. I did exactly that."

In his research on a Caribbean island called Bequia, in the Grenadines, Johnson (1986) explores the ways in which the Bequia male role in general, and the role of shipbuilder in particular, echoed his own gender socialization. Not only was he fitted into place by his informants, but he felt the fit, he wanted the fit, the fit involved his sense of self and his own biography. He describes his relation with a key informant, a master shipbuilder:

Men use tools to manipulate the elements and bring them under control, something I think men universally tend to admire in each other. Quite consciously, then, I sought to exhibit my [competence with tools]. . . . I remember feeling quite like a child trying to get my father's attention. I was a male coming to understand and trying to meet the gender expectations of a high-ranking male in order to acquire his approval. (Johnson, 1986, pp. 173-174)

Although gender roles in non-Western societies are often more restrictive than those in our own culture, there may be "deviant but acceptable" roles into which the anthropologist can be fitted. Rena Lederman found that the Mendi people of New Guinea "placed [her] in that 'deviant' female category reserved for ambitious, opinionated Mendi women with many . . . projects of their own apart from their husbands and with reputations for talking out loudly" (Lederman, 1986, p. 384). And in societies where myth and magic still permeate everyday life, mythic roles may be created for those fieldworkers who cannot be fit into prevailing cultural patterns. Laura Nader's (1986, pp. 104-105) behavior, outside the frame of traditional female, so puzzled the Zapotec Indians that they decided that she was able to turn herself into a man or woman at will. The Micronesians studied by Ann Fischer (1986,

p. 276) were afraid that if she wandered into areas where white faces were not a familiar sight she might be mistaken for a ghost, and attacked.

Androgyny and the honorary male. Women's invisibility in Western cross-gender settings, and immurement in women's worlds in the non-Western, have prompted some women fieldworkers to devise ways of gaining visibility and access within men's worlds. Typically, older women anthropologists are culturally androgynized, something that is particularly likely in cultures where older "native" women are allowed "male" privileges (Golde, 1986) while younger, unmarried women acquire the role of honorary male.[9] Or the fieldworker may attempt to foster ambiguity and obscurity in relation to her or his gender. Rena Lederman (1986, p. 378), for example, attempted to avoid existing gender roles among the Mendi, commenting that she was

> concerned with not aligning myself clearly with either the men or the women (as I understood the difference then) . . . I hoped to take advantage of whatever ambiguity my outsider status afforded, sidestepping the issue of my own gender and commitments for a while, if possible.

Androgyny, ambiguity, and honorary maleness within "primitive" cultures are associated with difference: with the racial, ethnic, and foreign stranger. Both whiteness and foreignness permit women fieldworkers more cross-gender behavior than that allowed to native women. Carolyn Fleuhr-Lobban (1986, p. 188) comments that in her fieldwork in the Sudan:

> As a woman with a husband and later a young daughter, I was not afforded the status of "honorary male" which many Western female professionals living alone in the Sudan receive [see below]. However, as a white female Westerner . . . engaged in research and attached to a family, my status was more ambiguous than Richard's, and as a result I had more social mobility in the system than he did. For example I could, if I wanted, sit with men alone or with my husband present.

Jean Jackson reports a different experience among the Takanoa of the Amazon. She found that after a period of time, "my femaleness had superseded my status as an affluent and high-status outsider" (Jackson, 1986, p. 271). She adds, "I was both elated and irritated. . . . Although more of an insider, I was being assigned to my proper place on the inside—second place" (p. 271).

Androgyny and honorary maleness are also reported in sociological fieldwork, particularly within male-dominated settings. Jennifer Hunt (1985) describes the various ways in which she attempted to become accepted in Western, gender-stratified world of urban police. There she had

> to convince police subjects that I was a trustworthy person who could conduct honest research I had to negotiate a gender identity that combined elements of masculine trustworthiness with feminine honesty. I therefore became a "liminal" person who dwelled between two opposing realms of the policeman's symbolic world. (Hunt, 1984, p. 286)

Hunt describes the urban police world as one dominated by a hierarchy of authority and a polarization of gender. Power relations are structured by the differentiation between elite (administrative) and street police, while

> gender is an essential aspect of identity . . . characterized by a structural and symbolic split between a feminine/domestic and a masculine/public domain . . . police distinguish between moral and non-moral persons, and between "clean" and "dirty" domains. These distinctions of morality and space are both mediated by gender. Thus superior moral virtue and honesty are perceived as feminine attributes of women who work in the "clean" world of the home. In contrast, corruption and dishonesty are viewed as masculine characteristics of men who work in the vice-ridden public sphere. In this case, the women of the home are viewed as untrustworthy in part because their superior feminine virtue is seen as dangerous in a public world in which most members are corrupt. In contrast, men who work on the street are perceived as trustworthy mainly because they share an involvement in illicit activity. (Hunt, 1984, p. 286)

Hunt claims not only a "liminal" or androgynous status but also a more situational negotiation of gender. At times, Hunt was the honorary male:

> Pistol practice provided the perfect opportunity to display the esteemed characteristics of masculine aggression and heart. One day I was practicing combat shooting and, as usual, my score was abominable. Ashamed, I left the range with my target hidden so no one could see it. However, a pistol instructor and several unknown off-duty officers approached and asked how I did. I responded, "not so good today, but tomorrow I'll blow the mother's guts out." Astonished, one officer

commented, "Did you hear what she said?!" They both smiled and nodded approvingly. I had shown that I was not a passive woman but a competent "man" who could feel just as violent as they. (Hunt, 1984, p. 290)

In other situations, shaped by the interactional dynamics of gender and authority in the police world, Hunt was a "dyke," "whore," "spy," "date," "crazy," or traditional woman:

> The feminine aspects of my gender identity were ritually restored in a [playful judo] game played with an academy instructor [in which Jennifer allowed herself to be overpowered]. . . . In this ritual, the sexual order of power was restored: the tough judo player was transformed into a weak and helpless woman. (Hunt, 1984, p. 239)

Despite her commitment to the rhetoric of negotiated gender (for which she provides no respondent-based evidence; she tells us only how she interprets the police view of her), Hunt returns in her analysis to a conventional "natural history" framework for understanding the achievement of trust as the acceptance of a negotiated researcher identity:

> The demonstration of membership [in the police world] involved two transformations. First, there searcher as subject was transformed from an untrustworthy to a trustworthy category of person. . . . Their culture no longer was characterized by a dichotomy between untrustworthy moral woman and trustworthy immoral man. Instead, it included the possibility of a new category of trustworthy street-woman-researcher and, by association, real woman cop. (Hunt, 1984, p. 293)

The fieldworker as spy. The presence of a stranger in a Burmese village or an urban police department may prompt host informants to share their lives with an honorary male or adopted child, but it can also provoke suspicions of spying. Both in the world of macropolitics— where CIA agents have become covert instruments of U.S. policies— and in the micropolitics of organizations—where the FBI or arm of local government may be seeking information—one place to which the fieldworker may be assigned is that of spy. And gender is one of the several features of the fieldworker and his or her task that elaborates the role of "spy." Depending upon the social and political context, a female stranger can be invisible (fieldworker as file clerk) or hypervisible (fieldworker as Mata Hari).

Although Hazel Hitson Weidman was eventually welcomed in the Burmese village she studied as a "daughter" and "benefactress," she later found that she had earlier been seen as a spy for the Burmese or the American government. (Weidman, 1986, p. 255). U.S. social scientists doing research in socialist countries such as Cuba (Fuller, forthcoming) and Rumania (Freedman, 1986) have also been suspected of spying either for the U.S. or the native government. And war or the threat of war can provoke fear that foreign anthropologists are spies. In the late 1930s in Brazil, Ruth Landes provoked suspicion that she was a spy in part because she lacked the obligatory cultural male patron-protector (1986, p. 126). She, in turn, found her actions the subject of Brazilian spying.

The relationship between gender and the suspicion of spying is a complex one. Since males are in most cultures perceived as more political, more linked to the sources of power, and more dangerous than females, they may be more readily taken for spies in situations of war or imperialism. Yet the sexualization of spying is associated with women, and with the potent cultural symbolism of Mata Hari—the snakewoman luring the hapless male into betrayal and doom. The literature on organizations indicates that a fieldworker whose gender does not fit with prevailing assumptions may be taken for a spy. Johnson (1986), for example, reports that in his study of elementary school teachers, all of whom were female, he was initially seen as a spy for the administration. Jennifer Hunt (1984) indicates that any stranger doing research on urban police is liable to definition as a spy, but a woman even more so. Not only was the police department she studied embroiled in a lawsuit charging gender discrimination against female officers, but also

> the role of spy was consistent with my gender identity. As a civilian and a moral woman I represented the formal order of law and the inside world of the academy. As both FBI and police internal security also represented the formal order, it was logical to assume I was allied with them. In addition, no policeman believed a woman was politically capable of fighting the department to promote honest research: Instead, the dominant elite would use me for their own purposes. (Hunt, 1984, p. 289)

The Body

The web of gender denotes not only one's place in the social structure but also the deep structures of human experience: body, sexuality, feelings, self. What is presented to the host culture is a body: a size and shape, hair and skin, clothing and movement, sexual invitation or untouchability. The embodied characteristics of the male or female fieldworker affect not only the place in the social order to which he or she is assigned, but also the fieldworker's and informants' feelings about attractiveness and sexuality, body functions and display. Some of the way in which the self is presented—such as hair style and clothing—can be altered; some—such as skin color and hand size—cannot. Thus the process of developing relationships in the field involves the monitoring and (perhaps) modification not only of behavior but also of the researcher's self: his or her body and its uses in the field.

Common fieldworker concern with body include general appearance, skin color, adornment, and dress. Douglas (1985) describes (what he sees as the impact of his) bodily appearance and demeanor when seeking "creative interviews" among "Goddesses" in Southern California. In rating the "body chemistry" that he claims to be significant in obtaining and conducting interviews, he says of himself,

> I happen to be fortunate in being largely nondescript chemically . . . most people don't seem to notice me in a crowd—just one more "normie," a middle aged man of medium height, slightly paunchy (these days), a bit bulbous headed and beady eyed (but not some extraterrestrial type) and a bit tanned and hacked in the face by time's bending sickle . . . I am not beautiful, sexy, otherwise exciting, or anything very distinct physically . . . I try to be fatherly-friendly, low-profile but warm, very uncritical and very sympathetic and appreciative. (Douglas, 1985, pp. 97-98)

Skin color is a crucial issue for anthropological fieldworkers, whose race or ethnicity is often different from that of their respondents. In a world where colonialism has left its mark on so many cultures, a fair skin and Caucasian physical characteristics set the anthropologist off not only as a foreigner, but also as someone of a higher status than the "natives." Fair skin is both attractive and distancing in the double status and relational systems within which postcolonial peoples live. Angrosino (1986, p. 65) defines skin color as part of the

> "dual socialization" [in] colonial societies. Members of such societies are typically taught to revere the behaviors and standards of the metropolitan power; this external value system is termed a system of respectability. . . . [But] they must still function in the local social networks: the system of indigenous values that orient a person's life is termed a system of reputation. . . . Actions, vocabulary, gestures, associations, styles of dress, of eating, of housing, types of personal relationships, and so forth, are all

clearly demarcated as to their respectable or reputable character, and the individual's social persona is evaluated in terms of which system's character predominates.

The value placed on light skin in many of the cultures studied by anthropologists is a reflection of the impact of Western cultural imperialism on the non-Western world. The white- or light-skinned person is the respectable one, the rich and powerful one, therefore the one desired and desirable. White, "foreign" female anthropologists, although they lack the superior status of males, acquire authority through association with the dominant, Western culture. Peggy Golde (1986, p. 79) found that her whiteness and appearance made her attractive to the Nahua:

> Fair skin was a highly prized attribute, and the girls who were considered most beautiful were all distinctly light-skinned. I also had curly hair, another much envied attribute, which symbolized white blood. And I was plump, a characteristic that further enhanced my desirability in their eyes.

Hazel Hitson Weidman (1986, pp. 255-256) had several characteristics that were considered desirable in Burmese women, including light skin and naturally arched eyebrows, but her "lean, angular" appearance and short hair made it difficult for the Burmese to determine her gender. Both Golde (1986) and Weidman (1986) found that their light skin and physical desirability partially offset the limits to research access imposed by being a stranger, a female, and a foreigner.

Social scientists designated "black" in our U.S. racial classification system have provided accounts of the varying significance of "ethgender" in the field. There are cultures and situations in which a dark skin color is desirable; Niara Sudarkasa was assigned the Yoruba role of "a child who has come home" on the basis of her status as a black American (1986, pp. 174-176).[10] But even in black cultures light skin maybe seen as preferable to dark. In describing his field work in Jamaica, black anthropologist Tony Larry Whitehead (1986) described his designation by the people of "Haversham" (the village he studied) as a "big, brown, pretty-talking man." "Big," as he comments, referred not to his size but to his presumed high status as an educated foreigner, while "pretty-talking" signaled his use of standard rather than dialect English. "Brown" was the term used by local Jamaicans to refer to that combination of light skin color, possession of material wealth, and "high morals" that symbolized status and respectability in the village. Whitehead (1986, p. 215) adds that

> my bigness and pretty talk caused numerous data collection difficulties at the beginning of my fieldwork. Lower-income males did not want to talk to me . . . they answered me with meaningless "yessirs," and "no sirs."

The fieldworker signals status and place by dress as well as skin color. In the late 1960s I was employed with several other graduate students in research involving the use of police records. Cordial relations with police officers at the various locations where we had to examine daily the records could be maintained only by strict conformity to conservative codes of dress and appearance for men and women. At that particular historical juncture, facial hair and long hair on males had come to symbolize political protest, student status, and youthful privilege in a combination enraging to those, such as police, who supported the Vietnam War, regarded students as effete draft dodgers, and resented what they saw as the simultaneous flouting and flaunting of upper-middle-class privilege. Thus males hired for the project had to cut their hair and shave, and wear jackets and ties rather than the frayed jeans and worn tennis shoes favored by graduate students at the time. Unlike skin color, dress and adornment are changeable and often must be changed, as generations of anthropologists have learned.

Sometimes the research task is facilitated by wearing clothes that are the same as one's hosts, sometimes not. Hazel Hitson Weidman (1986, p. 256) describes her adoption of the typical Burmese woman's style:

> I selected flowered [long robes] that appealed to their tastes, and I sat with propriety, as a modest, well-bred young woman should. I wore fragrant body lotion, lipstick, earrings . . . and flowers in my hair.

Although Friedl (1986, p. 212) did not emulate the dress of Greek village women, she did refrain from violating the norms against women smoking or wearing pants and shorts. Niara Sudarkasa, by contrast, found that in order to be able to ask questions in settings where the people did not already know her, she had to avoid dressing like a Yoruba woman. Yoruba women did not ask questions, and Niara (1986, p. 175) wanted to ask them:

> I was so often "accused" of being a Yoruba that when I went to a market in which I was not certain I would find a friend to identify me I made a point

of . . . dressing "like an American" . . . I even abandoned my sandals in favor of moderately high heels and put on make-up, including lipstick.

Different kinds of dress and hair style may be adopted to fit into the culture's gender roles, to disassociate oneself from the roles for some particular purpose, or to satisfy other demands based on age or social class. In their fieldwork in a Greek village, both Ernestine Friedl and her husband found that they were expected to wear certain clothes and avoid others. Since he was a professor, Robert was expected to dress daily in a suit and tie. Ernestine was allowed to dress less formally, but the villagers "drew the line at letting me wear a standard village woman's kerchief to guard against the sun, because that was clearly a symbol of the rural woman who works in the fields and I was allowed only partially to simulate the position of village women" (Friedl, 1986, pp. 213-214).

Modifications of the body itself are made by a variety of cultures. Scarring, nose and neck enlargement, footbinding, plastic surgery, clitoroidectomies, and circumcision have all been used to symbolize membership in a people, adherence to gender norms, proper adornment, or medical hygiene. The extensive literature on natives' body modifications by anthropologists contrasts with the lack of comment on their own conformity or nonconformity with these body norms and its research consequences. One exception is Oboler's (1986, p. 37) analysis of her husband's acceptance among the Nandi, and its bodily contingencies:

> his first trip to the river to bathe was a crucial test. In a spirit of camaraderie, as same-sex communal bathing is customary, he was accompanied by a number of young men. Tagging along was an enormous group of curiosity-seeking children and younger adolescents . . . everyone wanted to know the answer: . . . Was Leon circumcised? In Nandi, male initiation involving adolescent circumcision is the most crucial event in the male life cycle, without which adult identity, entry into the age-set system, and marriage are impossible. . . . Fortunately Leon, a Jew by ancestry and rearing, passed the test. I believe that an un-circumcised husband would have made fieldwork in Nandi extremely difficult for me.

While "female circumcision" (removal of the clitoris) was formerly practiced among the Nandi, it was rare at the time of the Oboler's (1986, p. 27) fieldwork, particularly among the educated. Carolyn Fluehr-Lobban (1986) notes that female circumcision was practiced extensively in the northern Sudan at the time she and her husband did their field research, despite governmental attempts to limit the practice. But she gives no indication of how her nonconformity to this deeply held and felt body norm affected her acceptance among the adult women she studied.

Gender norms encompass an enormous variety of expectations concerning what may legitimately be done to and with the body, where and when consumption of food and drink, washing and elimination of bodily wastes may be undertaken, and under what circumstances the body and its parts should be concealed or exposed. At the intersection of gender, body, and consumption are, in many cultures, rules concerning the intake of alcohol, tobacco, or other drugs. In both Western and non-Western cultures the customs of gender restrict women partly or completely from settings (such as ceremonial occasions, or bars) where liquor is consumed. While women anthropologists have a somewhat varied response to norms for dress and appearance, they seem almost uniformly to keep away from male-drinking locations (Golde, 1986). This is probably because of the common and cross-cultural association between male drinking and sexual license. A woman who goes drinking with men, in "their settings," opens herself up to sexual overtures.[11]

Sex

At the heart of male and female roles in any culture, shaping the adoption of and response to particular dress, perfumes, and hair styles, is the issue of sexuality. It is sexual behavior, after all, that ultimately sustains human society by ensuring its reproduction over time, and links one person to another through the kinship system. In some of the non-Western societies, this linkage is not only explicit but public; sexual relations, as well as marriage, are part of the civic discourse (Turnbull, 1986; Whitehead, 1986). In Western cultures—where some of the functional ties of kinship have been attenuated, and where intercourse is no longer necessarily tied to childbirth—sexuality is more often viewed as a private matter, although still subject to selective state regulation. The discourse of sexuality in the field has, I think, changed historically: from public silence outside "unpublished" diaries and correspondence (the 1920s to 1950s), to an examination of others' motivations, imputations, and unwanted overtures (the 1960s and 1970s), to a discussion (in the 1980s) of mutual sexual attraction and activity between fieldworkers and informants. This historical discourse on sexuality is itself a gendered one, with different female and male themes.

As indicated above, the question of sexuality in fieldwork first arose in the context of the safety from rape of "white women" alone in the field. There was little consideration among academics in the 1920s or 1930s of the possibility of the mutual attraction of a white woman scholar and her nonwhite male informants. But even in this era, in cultures where there was no legitimate role open to an unattached woman, locals might assign sexual motives to her. During her fieldwork in Brazil in the late 1930s, for example, Ruth Landes (1986, p. 137) was accused of seeking "vigorous" men to do more than carry her luggage. Indeed, Landes was labeled a prostitute during her research because of inadvertent violations of gender proprieties. On one occasion she checked into a hotel that, unknown to her, was frequented by prostitutes, while on another she wore a pair of shoes worn locally only by streetwalkers (1986, pp. 130-132). And returning to a Rumanian village as a widow and unattached woman, Diane Freedman (1986, p. 357) found that in contrast to her earlier fieldwork as a married woman

> my behavior was interpreted differently; friendly interactions were seen as indications of illicit behavior. My need for friendship and approval led me to participate in gatherings where cross-sex joking was common, and I was often the focus of the jokes. I interpreted these events on a surface level, as jokes in a friendly spirit. But the underlying theme was more serious than I realized at the time.

In both Western and non-Western cultures, some settings are more sexually focused than others; doing research in such settings implicates the researcher unavoidably in sexual imputations. In her studies of three Micronesian cultures, for example, Fischer (1986, p. 277) found that there were "no age limits beyond which an individual may freely carry on activities without having his [or her] motives suspected of being sexual." Researchers in Western cultures have encountered similar imputations when studying settings such as nude beaches (Douglas, Rasmussen, & Flanagan, 1977) massage parlors (Warren & Rasmussen, 1977) and homosexual settings (Styles, 1972; Warren & Rasmussen, 1977).

Social scientists who have studied sexual settings in our own culture tend to refer to others' imputations, but not to their own inclinations. Johnson (1976, p. 166) notes:

> Observers of all kinds have remarked about the strength and pervasiveness of sexual desire for aeons. . . . And yet when one reviews the

methodological writings in the social sciences, the implicit instruction is
to believe one of two things about this; either one must be a eunuch to
conduct scientific research, or . . . the desires of scientists involve only (or
primarily) cognitive elements. My research experiences . . . do not support
this view.

Even in writing about settings where 'sexual activity is fairly public,
fieldworkers have remained silent about their own sexual participation
or lack of it. In describing his research in a massage parlor, Paul
Rasmussen comments that this setting was both sexualized and
differentiated by gender roles, with men as customers, parlor owners
and boyfriends of the masseuses, and women as masseuses (who
provided sexual services for a fee), and girlfriends. As an attractive,
young male researcher, Rasmussen threatened the males in the setting,
the owners for financial and the customers and boyfriends for sexual
reasons. He dealt with the latter problem by "secretly" disclosing that he
was "gay" (he wasn't). Some of the masseuses, on the other hand,
wanted him as a boyfriend and consequently—he suspected—down-
played their sexual involvement in the massage scene when he interviewed them. He countered this problem by bringing in a woman
colleague to interview the masseuses. Throughout his discussion of these
research problems Rasmussen (Warren & Rasmussen, 1977, p. 363)
does not mention his own sexuality.

Like the massage parlors studied by Rasmussen, the nude beaches
explored by him and other research team members was a sexual setting,
although its gender relations seemed more egalitarian. He comments
that

> the nude beach scene is one of considerable sexual tension and display,
> although not necessarily in the form of overt sexual encounters.
> Newcomers to the scene hear a rhetoric of "naturalism and freedom,"
> while more seasoned participants learn to understand and negotiate the
> less apparent sexual dimensions of the scene. (Warren & Rasmussen,
> 1977, p. 354)

Women and men team members found that people on the nude beach
told them different things. Single men told Rasmussen about their
sexual interests, but provided the woman researcher (Flanagan) only
with the rhetoric of "freedom and naturalism." The reverse was true
when Rasmussen interviewed women and Flanagan interviewed men.

Interviewing couples on the beach raised the issue of jealousy if only one interviewer was used, so they learned to interview couples jointly (Warren & Rasmussen, 1977, pp. 354-355).

In those Western settings where sexuality is not the focus of activity, sociologists have been even more reticent about sex. Writing of his fieldwork in a social welfare office in Southern California in the late 1960s, John Johnson notes the absence of reported sexual activity between respondents and fieldworkers in methodological accounts, then comments on his own "affair with a social worker-informant" in the field. This affair, he adds, "produced a severe crisis for me personally and delayed the writing of the research reports" (Johnson, 1975, p. 166). Yet the affair did not, apparently, affect Johnson's place in the social welfare office he was studying, since in most settings in Western society sex is defined as a private activity without a ritual place in organizational work and public life.[12]

The only kind of ethnographic research in which there is a free expression of sexual interest and participation is in the area of homosexuality—in particular male homosexuality. The transition made by some homosexual individuals and groups from secrecy to overtness, a process that had its beginning in the gay liberation movement of the 1960s, is one root of this disclosure motif. The other is the nature of the gay world itself: a subculture in which sexuality and social order are fused, linking sexual activities and preferences to lifestyle, leisure, and—increasingly—work (including ethnographic work). One of the classics of the ethnographic literature on homosexuality, *Tearoom Trade*—first published in 1970—was written by a sociologist who did not then, but does now, avow his homosexuality openly.

Among the earliest sociological accounts of homosexual participation during field research is Joe Styles's "Insider/Outsider: Researching Gay Baths" (1979) a thoughtful analysis of the epistemology of participation and exclusion in ethnographic work. During his research in gay baths he went from an outsider to the sexual activities in the baths to a sexual participant (although his identity as a gay man remained the same throughout). He concludes that neither the "insider myth" that only inside participation can reveal "truth" nor the "outsider myth" of objectivity-as-discovery are useful ways of seeing ethnographic work. He comments:

Insider and outsider myths are not empirical generalizations about the relationship between the researcher's social position and the character of the research findings. They are elements in a moral rhetoric that claims exclusive research legitimacy for a particular group.... In reference to my own field work, the validity of this ... point should be self-evident. I did not possess any special access to the life of the baths merely because I am gay.... And even when I became a "real" insider, I still made errors.... If, as an insider, I did have some strange epistemologically privileged position, I cannot point to any of its manifestations, for I continued to make erroneous assumptions throughout the course of my field work. (Styles, 1979, pp. 148-149)

The fieldwork literature on mutual sexual attraction and sexual episodes seems to be predominantly a male literature, while the literature on sexual objectification and hustling appears to be almost entirely a female one. Women sociologists in ostensibly nonsexualized Western settings—from courtrooms to hospital wards—have in recent years reported encounters with respondents, often key informants, characterized by unwanted overtures. Sometimes these take the form of overt sexual propositions (Rovner-Pieckzenik, 1979) but more often women report overpersonalization of interaction (Warren, 1982) or the covert sexual hustle disguised as research cooperation (Gurney, 1985, p. 48).

Accounts of actual physical molestation occur not so much in the published literature as in the oral fieldwork folklore. One anthropological exception is Mary Ellen Conaway's (1986, p. 59) discussion of her fieldwork as a single woman among the Guahibo Indians of Venezuela, during which she was not only asked if she would have sex for money but was also physically molested:

I was mapping and identifying house types.... In the course of this work I met a Guahibo man, around sixty years of age, who delighted in sharing with me his life story and the history of the region. His wife had died a year earlier.... I departed ebullient—my first informant! After our third session, when I rose to depart, he extended his slight, four-foot-ten-inch frame and, quick as lightning, rubbed his nose across my clavical [sic]. I left disturbed. Future quick movement on my part prevented repetition of his affectionate behavior. (Conaway, 1986, p. 55)

Fieldwork done by Liz Brunner among the homeless of Los Angeles illustrates the contemporary salience of the problem of women's safety in the field.[13] During her fieldwork, Liz slept, drank, talked, and shared meals with the homeless on Los Angeles streets—almost all of whom were male. After several episodes of unwanted physical touching, she learned to avoid being alone with particular men, or going into dark areas of the street with those she did not know well. Like villagers in a "primitive" culture, these homeless men—some of them deinstitutional-ized mental patients—often did not share, or perhaps know about, Liz's Western middle-class, feminist values and beliefs concerning sexual expression and male-female relationships.

All societies have conceptions of what constitutes licit, and what constitutes illicit, sex. Cross-culturally, the legitimation of sexual activity has most often been through marriage, an institution that links the sexual to the social, the public to the private, and one generation to the next. Ethnographers have encounters with what the culture deems licit, as well as illicit, sexuality. Indeed, the typical experience of the unmarried, young female anthropologist—especially if she is made further desirable by foreignness, apparent wealth, light skin, and adoption of local dress and appearance norms—is to become the object of marriage proposals. In Peggy Golde's (1986, p. 80) research among the Nahua Indians, for example, she found herself the object of persuasion to

> marry in the village. . . . In trying to persuade me, they would argue that I wasn't too old for the marriageable boys of fifteen, sixteen or seventeen, since older women quite frequently married young boys. This was a patent untruth. Obviously they discounted my real age, twenty-nine, since in comparison with village women of the same age who had borne five or six children and worked in the fields, I looked much younger.

Although there are "corridor talk" accounts of anthropologists marrying their field informants, the literature is silent on the matter; only one case of a journalist posing as anthropologist and marrying in the field—Wynn Sargent—is on record.

Many societies legitimate—or perhaps even mandate—nonmarital sexual involvements. Accounts of culturally legitimate sexual partici-pation have been made by male rather than female fieldworkers (reflecting either conduct or conduct norms differentiated by gender). Among the Mbuti of Africa studied by Colin Turnbull, sexual conduct was a topic of lively interest, since it signaled not only marital intentions but one's place in the system of gender and age relationships. During his episodic research among the Mbuti, Turnbull reports that he was expected to engage in sexual relations during some of his assigned "gender age stages" but not others; as an adopted child and later as an elder he was defined culturally as asexual, but not during the "middle years" of youth and young adulthood when sexual nonparticipation was characteristic only of sorcerers. He describes the temporary sexual and emotional arrangement he made during this stage with a woman, Amina, which "satisfied the Mbuti as to the normality of my youthfulness and my ability to continue to live with them as a real youth, while it satisfied the villagers that I was not a sorcerer" (Turnbull, 1986, p. 25). Turnbull (1986, p. 19) also describes several fieldwork occasions when he refrained from sex

> when, as a philosophy graduate student with no training at all in anthropology I found myself in bed, in India, with a very attractive young Hindu girl who, because she called me "brother," expected nothing more [as did her parents] but tickling contests, I was able to respond in kind with a minimum of difficulty.... Similarly, having studied anthropology and on my way to the field for my first professional fieldwork, there was a natural "rightness" about the insistence of an extremely powerful Ndaka chief that I sleep with one of his daughters. But here I was in trouble, this time for medical rather than moral reasons, for I was simply not willing to take the risk: the old chief and his entire family were ridden with leprosy and yaws, as well as syphilis.

These varying experiences taught Turnbull about cultural expectations concerning male sexual behavior, and about the connections between sexual behavior, age, gender, and marriage during different phases of the life cycle. They also revealed aspects of his own nature: his ability to "turn off" sexual response under the influence of cultural demands for brotherly behavior, and other aspects of the self within there flexibility of fieldwork. He comments:

> What a wealth of ethnographic experience came from [the experience with Amina], from acting and reacting, from discovering all the time that there were larger selves hidden within me to which I need be true. There was also the joy and fullness that comes from deep human relationships, for without Amina it would have impossible for me to learn, as the Mbuti youth do, to fulfill my social obligations with respect to affection while fulfilling my personal life. (Turnbull, 1986, p. 25)

Among the accounts of heterosexual involvements in the field I could find only one by a woman researcher: Dona Davis's (1986) circumspect description of her affair with an engineer who had come to the

Newfoundland village she was studying to help with the installation of a water system. Since the norms of this Newfoundland community included a prohibition against premarital sex for women, she was worried about the effect on her research of staying overnight with this man. In fact, her behavior led to the discovery that this norm was not expected actually to govern conduct; in fact, "'having a boyfriend' or being 'paired off' seemed to make people a bit friendlier and more at ease around me" (Davis, 1986, p. 254). We can conclude from examining the field research literature on sexuality that its "pervasiveness" (Johnson, 1975) is not always reflected in the themes we ethnographers like to elaborate. We can also conclude, I think, something about the sex and gender norms of our own culture from reading the fieldwork literature. It is the male social scientists who write about the pervasiveness and power of sexual urges in a general rather than contextual or relational sense (see, for example, Johnson [1975] and Turnbull [1986]). And it is the male social scientists (still only a minority, of course, of all male social scientists) who tell us about their sexual experiences in the field. Whitehead and Price (1986, p. 294) note that

> the imbalance in treating sexuality issues . . . does not necessarily mean that these difficulties are more prevalent for male than for female fieldworkers. . . . there is a double taboo at work—sanctions against discussing sexuality publicly, particularly for women, and . . . sanctions . . . against public acknowledgement of factors that might undermine "objectivity" in the field.

Women social scientists, in contrast to men, seem more likely to discuss unwanted imputations and advances of a sexual nature than their own sexual desires, and stress marriage offers rather than proposals of a less licit nature. The one partial exception is the lesbian and gay fieldwork literature in which both women and men speak of their sexual relationships—but the women, still, more circumspectly. The discourse of sexuality, in our culture, is one subsumed within the more general discourse of gender.

The sexual politics of fieldwork. The historically situated experiences of sex and gender in fieldwork have recently given rise to a discussion of the sexual politics of fieldwork. At issue is the tradeoff between accepting sexism on the one hand and the acquisition of knowledge in the interest of furthering careers on the other. As I noted above,

Margaret Mead divided women fieldworkers into those concerned more with women's issues, and those focused on men. Women in the field also differ in the extent to which they are willing to be confined to gender roles, or treated as sexual objects, in the pursuit of information (compare Warren & Rasmussen [1977] with Easterday [1977]). Ann Fischer (1986, p. 279) points out that

> it is difficult for the American women field worker to adopt a womanly role in a culture in which women are subservient to men. . . . Professional women are not shrinking violets in their own societies, and they are not apt to become so just because the expectation exists in some other culture.

I suspect that the willingness to admit in print to an unprotesting acceptance of sexist treatment is also historically and biographically variable. In my fieldwork, in contrast to my academic life, I did not find the "shrinking violet" role particularly problematic; indeed, I used to enjoy wearing different masks in the field.[14] Other women, however, have found the sex-gender-knowledge tradeoff to be both personally and politically distasteful (Easterday et al., 1977). What can be seen on the one hand as women's special talent for fieldwork (see below) can be seen on the other as a feature of the politics of gender dominance and submission that characterize so many cultures.

Women fieldworkers in male-dominated organizations have experienced several dimensions of male dominance: not only sexual hustling, but also assignment to traditional female roles and tasks such as mascot, go-fer, audience, butt of sexual or gender joking, or "cheerleader" (Easterday et al., 1977; Gurney, 1985; Kanter, 1977; Rovner-Pieczenik, 1976; Warren, 1972). The female fieldworker, like

> the female professional in a male-dominated organization is a token, and her continued presence in the setting may be contingent upon passing certain loyalty tests, including ignoring derogatory remarks or allowing her gender to provide a source of humor for the group. (Gurney, 1985, p. 44)

I described some of these types of interaction above, in my discussion of gender, sex, and research relations. But what is missing in my published account and many others (Wax, 1979) is the response to sexist treatment. As Gurney (1985, p. 56) notes:

We are rarely told how the researcher responded to [sexual hustling]. We also are not told how the female researcher felt about her response to the incident, whether she was satisfied that she did the correct thing under the circumstances or was uncomfortable with her own actions . . . we are given a picture of the setting that is very one-sided. The [female] researcher comes to be seen as a passive recipient of actions by setting members rather than an active participant in the interaction. Therefore, although we are learning more about the types of difficulties female researchers encounter in the field, we are not learning much about how to respond to them.

What shapes response is the tradeoff between harmonious research relations in the field (based on the pursuit of knowledge and of career advancement) and the typically feminist politics of fieldworkers in academia (based on the struggle to overcome sexism). In addition, the pervasive gratitude often felt by researchers toward those who have allowed access to their worlds can hamper a more militant response. Like Gurney (1985, p. 56), I have found that in my fieldwork

> my tolerance of sexism was based upon my gratitude toward setting members . . . and my concern with maintaining rapport. . . . I often wished I were a more militant feminist who could lecture the staff on their chauvinism and insensitivity and change their attitudes toward women. Instead I was always the polite and courteous researcher who tolerated much and said little. I occasionally wondered if I was betraying my beliefs and values, but I allowed it to continue.

Reluctance to discuss sex, or fear of the consequences to one's own career of describing sexual episodes (Gurney, 1985), are two of the reasons that stories of serious sexual hustles remain confined to oral folklore, but they are not the only ones. Women anthropologists have described episodes of unwanted sexual advances from the people they were studying, and indicated that they refrained from public discussion of these episodes on grounds of self-blame, gratitude, or political commitments. If the episode occurred in the context of the anthropologist's violation of known local gender codes, then she felt it was "her fault," and she "asked for it." And even if this was not the case, the anthropologist felt not only gratitude for the cooperation of the people and an unwillingness to discredit them on this ground, but also a more generalized unwillingness to discredit "primitive" peoples oppressed by colonialism and modernism.[15] Some of the same kinds of political concern have been voiced by sociologists studying racial or social class groups whom they perceive similarly as oppressed; indeed, there is often a general avoidance of reporting any sorts of "bad behavior" black, lower-class, or non-Western men might engage in, from unwanted sexual advances to drinking and carousing (Whitehead, 1986).

The politics of fieldwork reflects not only a commitment to oppressed peoples, but also a lively concern with one's own career as an academic. Such a concern may itself lay the groundwork for the development of gender myths in fieldwork, myths that may reflect more the norms of academia than the culture of the field. Gurney (1985), for example, challenges the rosy view of women as more adept than men at creating and maintaining rapport with respondents in the field (see below). She asserts that being female can result in a lack of credibility in the presentation of research, which in turn promotes concealment of fieldwork problems:

> A female researcher may not discuss the issue of gender in presenting her fieldwork experience for a variety of reasons. . . . [She] may overlook or even deny difficulties she experienced in the field to avoid having her work appear unsound. Any lapse in rapport with setting members may cast doubt on the information she received from them. There is also the added embarrassment of acknowledging that one's status as a female over-shadowed one's identity as a female. (Gurney, 1985, p. 44)

During her own research in a prosecutor's office, Gurney (1985, p. 45) "overlooked incidents which [others] regarded as sexist" because of her discomfort with the idea that her work might have been compromised because of her gender. It was only later that she came to define the problems she had had in the field as related to her gender, rather than other factors such as youth and inexperience. It would be interesting to know whether the myth of the special talents of women for fieldwork is based at least in part on the concealment of problems in published accounts.

A second aspect of the politics of gender in fieldwork is related to a feminist commitment to research that involves benefits to or connections with other women. There has been a general movement in both sociology and anthropology, animated by a socialist, humanist, or religious concern for the plight of the world's oppressed people, to engage in research only if there is the probability of some outcome beneficial to the people studied. Feminists whose politics are linked to these movements but focused on women are interested in linking their research activities to succor for women in our own and other cultures. For example, during the course of their research on battered women, Kathleen Ferraro and John M. Johnson founded and helped to raise funds for a shelter for battered women (Ferraro, 1983). Similar action research agendas occur in fieldwork or interviewing of rape victims and victims of child abuse and molestation.

Recent women's anthropology has been informed by a political ideology of cross-cultural female solidarity and mutuality of experience. Strathern (1984) distinguishes between feminist anthropology and anthropological feminism. The aim of feminist anthropology is to build a subdiscipline contributing to the discipline's (and the subdiscipline's practitioners') advancement. But the aim of anthropological feminism, she says, is to create a feminist community whose premises and goals are in opposition to those of anthropology: historically specific conflict and identity building replace notions of generalization, science, and androcentric consensus. Anthropological feminism is one aspect of anthropology's recent experimentation with ethnographic form; it is "trying to shift discourse, not improve a paradigm" (Rabinow, 1986, p. 255):

> that is, it alters the nature of the audience, the range of readership, and the kinds of interactions between author and reader, and alters the subject matter of conversation in the way it allows others to speak—what is talked about and whom one is talking to. (Strathern, 1984, p. 338)

An example of this feminist-revisionist ethnographic genre is Marjorie Shostak's *Nisa: The Life and Words of a !Kung Woman* (1981). The ethnographer's and the respondent's relationship is one of mutual transference and transformation; as Clifford (1986: 107) says of the story, it

> is part of a new interest in revaluing subjective (more accurately intersubjective) aspects of research. It emerges from a crucial moment of feminist politics and epistemology: consciousness raising and the sharing of experience by women. A commonality is produced that, by bringing separate lives together, empowers personal action, recognizes a common estate. This movement of recent feminist consciousness is allegorized in Nisa's fable of its own relationality. (In other ethnographies, traditionally masculine stories of initiation and penetration differently stage the productive encounter of self and other.)

Thus the sexual politics of fieldwork moves historically from a concern with sexuality and sexism in male-female field relationships to a more pervasive concern for the threading of gender into the heart of knowledge and praxis.

3. GENDER AND KNOWLEDGE

As I indicated above, accounts of sex and gender in the field may be framed in the language of rapport, or they may be analyzed epistemologically. In this section, methodological accounts are taken *as* accounts, to be read for that web of gender that occurs in the production of discourse rather than in the recounting of anecdotes. The contemporary epistemology of gender in social science has moved from analytic concerns with feminist theory (about settings) to rhetorical concerns with discourse analysis (about the transformation of settings into knowledge through social science categories), and the reading of fieldwork documents—from field notes to ethnographies—as literary texts.

There is a lack of explicit connection, in my own and others' methodological accounts, between anecdotes of the field on the one hand and presentational strategies on the other. We are told, for example, that Carolyn Fleuhr-Lobban, as a married woman, was treated to oil massages, and we are told that rapport was enhanced for Dona Davis by taking a lover. The implication—sometimes the explicit indication—is that the events described in these anecdotes resulted in greater rapport, which in turn resulted in access to more (and presumably more truthful) information. Besides the very real possibility that there may be situations in which tension, conflict, and a lack of rapport might produce more (truthful) information, what is missing in this interactionist sequence is the semiotic: the process through which interactions are reproduced as knowledge—as analytic categories, as field notes, as ethnographies. Instead of the weaving of connections between experience and the production of knowledge, recently, ethnographers (including myself) tend to produce and maintain various mythologies, including that of "women's place" in fieldwork methodology.

Women's Place in Fieldwork Methodology

Just as women are defined as occupying a certain, gendered place in a given culture, they appear in the fieldwork literature in particular ways.

And these ways have changed over time. To illustrate, I want to consider briefly the place of gender in the methodological accounts of the Chicago school fieldworkers, and, in particular, in a recently published 1920s essay by Paul Goalby Cressey (1986). In the fieldwork (or case study) literature of the early Chicago school, neither gender nor many other methodological issues were seen as especially problematic. Although there is one textbook on field methods from that era (Palmer, 1928) there are few other surviving methodological analyses (Bulmer, 1983, p. 95). Cressey's "Comparison of the Roles of the 'Sociological Stranger' and the 'Anonymous Stranger' in Field Research," typically, discusses gender only in the more general context of research role. Using a theoretical framework derived from Simmel's analysis of "the stranger," Cressey describes the relationships he and other members of his research team (a woman and a Filipino man) experienced in the taxi dance halls they were studying. As in Simmel's original analysis, Cressey's "stranger" seems to be, both explicitly and implicitly, a male stranger. As Cressey put it:

> Simmel lays particular emphasis upon the fact that the "stranger" is a product of mobility in that he is physically present yet culturally distant from the group—and yet a part of it. Likewise, Simmel emphasizes the enhanced freedom from sentiment and the folkways and mores of the group, and the increased "objectivity" that results. . . . But the contribution of Simmel to our specific problem is found in a special suggestion of his. He points out that in the relation of the "stranger" to the group he has opportunity to gain surprising "confessional" rapport with the others of the community. (Cressey, 1983, p. 104)

Grammatically, the stranger is explicitly a "he." Historically, Simmel's analysis was developed in the context of a society in which strangers—male traders and migrants thrown up on the shores of urbanization and modernization—were coming to be commonplace. And Simmel's and Cressey's ideal typical stranger partakes epistemologically of many of the traits associated with maleness (Keller, 1985): freedom from sentiment and from the mores and folkways, and objectivity within a web of subjectivity. But, ironically, that characteristic of the stranger portrayed as most useful to understanding the methodology of fieldwork is one associated in the contemporary fieldwork literature with femaleness—the ability to communicate and gain "confessional rapport."

Cressey's essay alerts us to the possibility that this view of women's special place in fieldwork may be more historically determined than universal; more a feature of discourse than a social fact. He saw the male bond, rather than the characteristics associated with women, as the basis for a "confessional" relation between the sociological stranger and "his" respondent, commenting that

> it may be said that the "anonymous confessional relationship" is a mono-sexual grouping. Its most striking instance is in the relationship of two men, although to a lesser extent the same dyadic grouping may exist between two women. Such anonymous confidential relationship may exist between a man and a woman, although perhaps less frequently and less completely. (1983, p. 110)

Cressey provides some details about gender and "ethgender" in the taxi dance hall research, supporting his general hypothesis concerning fieldwork rapport and the male bond. He worked with a "young woman student" to try to gain interview rapport with the taxi dance hall hostesses, but

> before long it was apparent that she could not establish rapport with the girls. She might engage them in a brief conversation, but none of the girls were interested in continuing these confidences. (Cressey, 1983, p. 112)

Although he attributes the lack of rapport in part to the woman researcher's moralizing attitude, Cressey assumes unproblematically that men are more likely to achieve rapport with respondents than women.

Cressey also collaborated with a male Filipino coworker whom he used to gain interviews with the Filipino male clientele of the taxi dance hall. Although this young man was able to talk to the Greek proprietors of the dance halls—who were in general prejudiced against Filipinos—they would talk only about money and their ownership, not about the "girls." Sexual topics were taboo between the representatives of what were then defined as more and less stigmatized ethnic groups (Cressey, 1983, p. 108).

Since the 1920s the special features and problems of women's place in culture and in fieldwork have given rise to a mythology of women's particular contributions to the fieldwork enterprise. This special place assigned to women is based on women's general social place as nurturers, communicators, emotional laborers, and—as a muted undertone—sexual objects. It is almost a truism of interview research, for example, that in most situations women will be able to achieve more "rapport" with respondents because of their less threatening quality, and better communication skills. Male interviewers are considered preferable only for highly restricted topics such as police work and then only in relation to male respondents.

Although women may sometimes be prevented from entering male worlds, they may nevertheless encounter more willingness on the part of both males and females to allow access to inner worlds of feeling and thought. Female fieldworkers seem at once less threatening and more open to emotional communication than men (Codere, 1986; Golde, 1986; Whitehead & Conaway, 1986). Both in sociology (Douglas, 1979) and in anthropology, fieldwork has been associated with women, and quantitative work with men. Laura Nader (1986, p. 114) summarizes:

> Women make a success of field work because women are more person-oriented; it is also said that participant observation is more consonant with the traditional role of women. Like many folk explanations there is perhaps some truth in the idea that women, at least in Western culture, are better able to relate to people than men are.

Both the ideology of better communication skills and a trading in female sexuality are, I think, implicated in the contemporary mythology of women fieldworkers' use as "sociability specialists," "opening up" situations and respondents, and generally smoothing the path for male members of fieldwork teams. As Douglas (1976, p. 214) comments:

> In most settings, the ultimate sociability specialists are women. These low-key women do not threaten either the women or the men. They are liked by and commonly share intimacies with both sexes. Men are simply more threatening to both sexes, even when they are the most sociable.

In their study of the nude beach (Douglas et al., 1977), Douglas and Rasmussen eventually employed Carol Ann Flanagan, a woman they met on the beach, as a sociability specialist and coauthor.

This blend of the nurturing and sexual facets of women's place in the social order and in fieldwork is particularly evident in settings where sexuality is a focus (such as the nude beach study) but is also relevant to settings such as formal organizations where sexuality remains an undercurrent to the bureaucratic business at hand. In my research in the mental health court I found that the judge's sponsorship of me, and his willingness to share information with me—and indeed force my presence on others in the setting, which he had the power to do—was premised almost entirely on his wish to engage in daily flirtations. I was a sexualized "mascot" not only to this aging judge but also to several of the other men in the setting, who were pleased to parade in and out of the courtrooms and chambers with me in tow (Warren, 1982).

Woman's traditional nurturing role, associated with mothers rather than sexual partners, can also come into play during the fieldwork process, in the various bargains, gifts, and exchanges fieldworkers and their hosts come to share. In my research in the drug rehabilitation center (Warren, 1972), for example, I often volunteered, and came to be expected to perform household chores along with the residents, including cooking meals and cleaning up. Although in theory this organization was nonsexist in its household labor—newcomer rather than woman was the status associated with cooking and cleaning up—in practice it was almost always the women who performed these chores. Male fieldworkers, by contrast, are typically asked to perform "male" maintenance tasks, or serve as liaisons with bureaucracies (see, for example, Johnson, 1975; Oboler, 1986).

The generalizations found in the social science literature concerning the "advantages and disadvantages" of women versus men in fieldwork also reflect women's place in their own social order. Besides their restriction to particular worlds within settings, women fieldworkers are portrayed as more accessible and less threatening than men; coupled with their "superior" communicative abilities, this makes the inter-actions of fieldwork generally easier (Fischer, 1986; Golde, 1986; Mead, 1986; Warren & Rasmussen, 1977; Wax, 1979). Women are more likely to be protected by their host communities, which in some cases (for example, police work) can result in less rather than more access to information (Golde, 1986; Warren & Rasmussen, 1977). Although the fieldworkers who write about the different experiences of women and men are careful to note that these generalizations depend on the purposes and methods of the study, the host culture, and the other characteristics of the fieldworker (such as age and marital status), there is a remarkable cross-cultural similarity in these portrayals, from the Eskimo to New Guinea, and from New England in the 1960s to Los Angeles in the 1970s.

Objectivity and emotions in field research. Another special contribution that women are said to have made to contemporary fieldwork is in bringing back into focus the emotional as well as cognitive aspects of social research. As Evelyn Fox Keller (1985) points out, science has been historically identified with rationality, objectivity, cognition, and the mistrust of emotion—"traits" also associated with men. Women, on the other hand, have been identified with irrationality, subjectivity, and emotionality, all anathema to "proper" science and social science. It is within fieldwork and the development of an ethnographic tradition that the emotional as well as the cognitive dimensions of social research have become an important focus of scholarly attention.

In the social science of the 1920s through the 1950s, a stance of objectivity and rationality was still the aim of fieldworkers as well as of more statistically oriented social scientists (Thomas, 1983). Indeed, older social scientists, such as Margaret Mead, writing in their later years, cautioned against what they saw as the increasing "emotionalism" of the field in general, and particularly women (Mead, 1986). The "proper" expression of feelings was not in the published ethnography or even in the field notes, but in such "private" texts as diaries and letters; even there, the expression of feelings could provoke dismay, as did Malinowski's private diaries when they were published in 1967 (Mead, 1986, pp. 324, 324n). Today, however, there has been a renewed substantive as well as methodological interest in the role of emotions in social life, which has resulted in the reevaluation of the interrelationship of gender, feeling, and rationality in science and social science (Hochschild, 1983; Keller, 1985).

Social scientists have increasingly come to take seriously the presumption that findings and methods are interdependent, and that feelings as well as ideas guide research design, procedures, relationships, and analysis. The day-to-day work of research in any settings involves feelings of like and dislike, boredom and annoyance, fear and shame. And some research brings the researcher face to face with profound experiences of birth or death, aging or pain. Barbara Katz Rothman (1986, pp. 50-52), for example, describes the guilt and grief associated with her research on amniocentesis and abortion in the context of her own recent motherhood:

> I had no idea how much pain was there, or how much pain I would suffer. . . . I was so close, emotionally and physically, to the pregnancy experience, to the terrible, urgent intimacy of that relationship. And [my]

baby—I loved her so passionately, so fiercely. . . . It was partly survivors' guilt. . . . The constant going back and forth, between these women and their grief . . . and my love for my healthy baby—it tore at me, but it made me try to understand the meaning of mother love.

These profound emotions changed the course of Katz Rothman's research. She hired a research assistant—a young woman who had no children—to continue the interviewing with those whose amniocentesis had resulted in an abortion. And she came to interpret amniocentesis and abortion not simply as medical events but as the death of a baby, with all the pain that entails for a woman and mother.

The core of the process described by Katz Rothman is countertransference: Emotions are evoked in the fieldworker while listening to respondents' accounts of their own lives. Fieldwork, like any interaction of everyday life, evokes the whole range of feelings associated with everyday life. But transference or identification—in fieldwork as in everyday life—is evoked mainly through talking with others, in conversations, or (as with Katz Rothman's research) interviews. While psychiatrists and psychologists locate the origins of identification (that of client with counselor) and counteridentification (that of counselor with client) in early familial childhood experiences, social scientists see them as rooted also in current roles and experiences and in the social structure (Warren, 1987). In her interview study of working-class women and men, for example, Rubin (1976) found that the process evoked for her her own working-class origins along with her later Marxist, feminist, and therapeutic commitments. The resulting analysis, the book *Worlds of Pain,* reflects not only the respondents' lives but also Rubin's identification with their pain.

Feminist Theory and Discourse Analysis

Since the 1960s, feminist scholars have been developing a gendered view of social life and social science. Feminist theory seeks to direct social science analysis toward issues and interpretations focused on gender. Discourse analysis—the meta-analysis of data analysis—makes problematic the grounds of analysis itself; feminist discourse analysis turns scholarly attention to a number of formerly taken-for-granted androcentric features of scientific writing. And, closing the hermeneutic circle, some scholars have recently come to question the assumptions of their own feminist theory and discourse.

In sociology, the development of feminist theory has paralleled an increasing disciplinary interest in historical, comparative, and qualitative styles of research. One implication of this development is that feminist sociologists integrate their fieldwork into feminist-structuralist rather than feminist-ethnographic analysis. An example of a study that uses ethnographic work to develop feminist theory is Arlie Hochschild's *The Managed Heart: Commercialization of Human Feeling* (1983). Although she uses interviews and participant observation with Delta Airlines stewardesses as data, Hochschild's intent is not to provide us with an ethnography of everyday life at Delta Airlines. Rather, it is to give the reader a sense of the subjective experience of emotional labor within a capitalist society in which even feelings are for sale. In short, it is a feminist critique of our current social order.

While feminist theory frames social life in a gendered context, discourse analysis turns the feminist gaze, reflexively, upon the rhetorical structure of social science itself. Discourse analysis has had a long history within the philosophy of science, but it is only recently that it has gained a more general legitimacy within the social and natural sciences as they are daily produced. In the social sciences, discourse analysis has focused on the ways in which rhetorical devices provide demonstrations of objectivity, facticity, and quantifiability (Gusfield, 1976), and on the embeddedness of all analysis within the observer's biography and historical location (Barham, 1984; Rubin, 1979; Warren, 1987). And not only in the social but also in the natural sciences, one allied theme has been the place of gender in the construction of disciplinary rhetorics. As Evelyn Fox Keller (1985, p. 8) notes, the history of discourse in science involves the construction of a "science-gender system" in which "ideologies of gender and science inform each other in their mutual construction."

Discourse analysis in science takes note of the fact that in both the natural and the social sciences, knowledge "has been produced by a particular subset of the human race—that is . . . white, middle class males" (Keller, 1985, p. 7). Thus the symbolic meanings attributed to white males and valued by them also become attached to the scientific enterprise, notably "the deeply rooted popular mythology that casts objectivity, reason and mind as male and subjectivity, feeling and nature as female" (Keller, 1985, p. 6). Science has developed by obscuring the personal and the emotional origins of knowing:

> Our "laws of nature" are more than simple expressions of the results of objective inquiry or of political and social pressures, they must also be

read for their personal—and by tradition, masculine—content. (Keller, 1985, p. 10)

Feminist discourse analysis "uncovers . . . the personal investment scientists make in impersonality; the anonymity of the picture they produce is revealed as a kind of signature" (Keller, 1985, p. 10). Since the 1920s it has generally been women scholars—whether avowedly feminist or not—who have come to recognize the implicit assumption that what is important about society is what the men are up to. From her research in Pacific cultures in the 1930s and 1940s, anthropologist Camilla Wedgwood (1957, p. 495) concluded:

> It is sometimes assumed unwittingly that the males play the dominant role in social change and that for a study of acculturation the effects of culture contact on the females are relatively unimportant. The effects on the lives and outlooks of the females are less obvious, less direct, and usually less easy to analyze, but we cannot assume that they are less important.

Contemporary anthropologists have continued to research the male bias in the discipline, using the work of Malinowski and his students as examples. Annette Weiner challenged Malinowski's interpretation of Trobriand Island culture:

> Weiner believes that Malinowski, like other scholars, placed too much emphasis on individualistic and utilitarian concerns—for example the seeking of political alliance and power—and consequently neglected systems of exchange that involve women and are related to a society's sense of intergenerational community. . . . "There is a great deal of truth in what Malinowski says," observed Weiner, "but he was trapped by his own sense of what women were about." (Sass, 1986, p. 56)

What Malinowski overlooked was the meaning and significance of women's activity as cultural ritual, something that he saw only in male activity. Malinowksi and others had established the importance of reciprocal gift exchanges in the public life of Trobriand Islanders, but had assumed that Trobriand women made no such exchanges, since they were confined to the domestic sphere. By contrast, Weiner established the existence of a female exchange ritual that was "a linchpin [sic] of Trobriand social and cultural life" (Sass, 1986, p. 57).

Similar challenges to the prevailing definition of the situation have been made by contemporary feminist sociologists. The classic sociologists, Marx, Weber, and Durkheim, all focused their theories around concepts of the division of labor that excluded the spheres particular to women: their reproductive, household, and emotional labor. Both mainstream and Marxist sociology in the United States ignored the productive tasks of women partly because they were unpaid and partly because they took place in the domestic sphere. Not only the functionalist or Parsonian but even the critical or conflict theories of social order take male activities as their causal principle and as the source of social change.

Feminist theory and discourse analysis have affected mainstream social science, making it more aware of the historical determinants of both social life and social science. Feminist theory (as an interpretive frame for data) has challenged traditional Marxist class analysis, just as current theories of the state and its hegemony have affected Marxist economic determinism. Feminist discourse analysis (as an interpretive frame for interpretive frames) has made scholars aware of both the surface (as in the use of the word *man* for human) and the deeper reflexive structures of rhetoric.

The basic presuppositions of social science theories, derived historically from a philosophical tradition, are gendered presuppositions—as Evelyn Fox Keller (1985) notes, it is, after all, white male Westerners who have been responsible for the developing language of philosophy and science. As an example from ethnographic theory (and I present this not as a definitive example or criticism, but as a way of beginning a dialogue), Michael H. Agar (1986, p. 24), in another volume in this series, describes the contribution made by the philosopher Alfred Schutz to the development of phenomenological and ethnographic perspectives:

A person, living in a world endowed with meaning, has at any given moment an interest at hand. For our purposes, the interest at hand will be called a *goal*, of which the person may or may not be conscious. The goal of the moment is not an isolated entity; rather, it is part of a larger system of goals in a person's world. . . . The actor, with goal at hand, sketches out a plan of action based on anticipation and expectations in the stock of knowledge available.

Aside from the obvious Western cultural assumptions in Agar's rendition of Schutz (the notion of the unconscious, the systems perspective), the very emphasis on goals as the wellspring of social action seems to me to be premised on men's experience of the world—at least Western men whose generational membership spans roughly the era of Schutz to Agar. In an interview study I did as a graduate student I investigated academic women's experience of their career trajectories. I was interested in finding out whether or not other women's experience had been like mine: characterized not so much by goals and planning, but by drift, and response to circumstances. I found that for these late 1960s-early 1970s women professors even the purportedly goal-organized career path of academia had indeed—and especially in the earlier stages—been characterized by drift and adaptation rather than goals, planning, and choice. They described entering graduate school in terms such as getting away from their household "duties," or having nothing else to do in the college town where their husbands had chosen to teach. They—we—had been brought up to adapt to circumstances, often to men's plans, rather than to make plans and seek goals.[16]

Although the presuppositions of ethnography are not free from the structuring of consciousness by social place (indeed, no discourse is), fieldworkers have always been aware of the reflexive nature of knowledge. This awareness derives, I think, from the face-to-face nature of the method itself, which hinders the positivistic retreat into the myths of objectivity and "any person" research. Indeed, among the canons of the qualitative approaches in the social sciences are the unity of the knower and the known, and the dependence of the findings on the procedures used in discovering. But it is only very recently that the significance of gender and other aspects of reflexivity in the field has entered the mainstream of academic discourse. And it is even more recently that fieldwork reflexivity has itself become the object of analysis. Attention has turned in the social sciences to our own discourses as they reveal the textual interaction of self and other.[17]

Fieldwork as Text

Fieldwork accounts have recently come to be seen as texts revealing not so much "the setting" as the interpretive moment; thus gender is analyzed not only as it shapes the processes and presuppositions, but also the productions of fieldwork. These productions include field notes, methodological accounts, and published research monographs and articles. In anthropology, feminism, the use of others' field notes over time, and a renewed attention to methodology have combined to produce an interest in field notes as text. Smith (1986, p. 2) notes somewhat cynically that "the current concern with text, meaning, writing and reflexivity is as much to be accounted for by its domination of western intellectual life in the 1980s as by its relevance to the ethnographic enterprise per se," but goes on to discuss his own use of the field notes of an "anthropologist housewife," then Ella Embree, some forty years earlier. The exercise of using others' field notes, removed in time, place, and sometimes gender, has made anthropologists increasingly aware of their biographical and historical features. As Nancy Lutkehaus (forthcoming, a) says of her use of Camilla Wedgwood's field notes from the 1930s:

> My initial reading of Wedgwood's fieldnotes—as well as letters to her friends, mentors and families and her journals from the field—captivated my attention less for their data about Manam society and culture than for what they could tell me about Wedgwood herself. Like Wedgwood, I was a woman and I was also, like her, going into the field alone. Because of the nature of her experience, I identified with her . . . I tried to read between the lines, searching for clues as to what a similar experience 45 years later might hold in store for me.

Lutkehaus not only used Wedgwood's field notes from the Manam research, she also did her own fieldwork in New Guinea. She concludes that the differences she found in the culture could be explained not only by historical change between the 1930s and 1980s but also by the ways in which she and Wedgwood interpreted the interactions they observed. Where Wedgwood "found" the relationship between married women and men to be basically cooperative and harmonious, Lutkehaus "saw" it as fundamentally conflictful (Lutkehaus, 1982, pp. 36-41). She asks:

> How are we to reconcile these two disparate sets of information about male-female relations in Manam society? . . . Is Manam society accurately portrayed by the description of gender ideology but expresses difference but not dominance? (Lutkehaus, 1982, p. 41)

From a rhetorical or textual perspective, the locus of reconciliation would lie not in the "nature" of Manam society but in the biography and history of anthropological interpretation.

Field notes may be reinterpreted not only by others but also by the person who wrote them. Biographical change occurs in the context of historical change, and people come to think differently about their own interpretations. Wolf (1986) describes her field research in China as an anthropologist's wife in the 1950s, and her later reinterpretation of her own field notes. As did Ella Embree in Japan, Wolf took notes "for her husband," mainly on the life of the women, from which he was excluded. During the 1960s and 1970s she underwent two transformations: She became an anthropologist and a feminist. These changes led her to what she calls an "engendering" of her earlier field notes, an emerging awareness of the significance of the world of the women of China, and of the nature of their power.

> The Chinese family as an institution has been [characterized as] . . . a male-dominated structure. . . . The consensus seemed to be that Chinese women [were] . . . of minimal interest in examining the Chinese family's strengths, cycles or romance. . . . I was vaguely aware of this at the time of my first fieldwork in Taiwan, but since my relationship to academia at that time was purely marital, I did not feel constrained by that paradigm. I hung out with the women as did all women, and the perspective I developed on the family was theirs. When I began to write about the Chinese family I . . . began the struggle at which I was ultimately defeated to make my field notes conform to that paradigm. They would not. (Wolf, 1985, p. 7)

Wolf's account of her China field notes gives us insights into the nature of the relationship between biography and interpretation in historical context. She notes that her analytic problems with the androcentric paradigm of the Chinese family were at first "vague," since there were no disciplinary guidelines in the 1950s (nor did she have disciplinary involvement) for making a gender-based critique. Once she became an anthropologist rather than a wife of one, and in the context of a resurgence of feminism, she was able to write in a new way about the women in the Chinese family.

The gendering of field notes is a reflection both of the differential experiences of men and women in the field, and (perhaps) their ways of reflecting back upon experience. Where it has been possible to make comparisons, as in husband-wife anthropological teams, there are indications that the different ways in which females and males are defined and treated are reflected in different field notes. Ann Fischer (1986, p. 282) says of her and her husband's fieldwork on the island of Truk, in Micronesia:

> There was a marked contrast between the treatment of myself and my husband. When he visited me, my chair (the only one on the island) would

be preempted for his use, and an informant would squat by his side, spending hours answering his questions. Formal arrangements would quickly be made to demonstrate for him some aspect of Trukese life in which he had expressed an interest. As a result, if our field notes are compared, my husband's record is of the more formal aspects of culture in exactitude, while mine tend to be a running account of what was happening in the village or in the homes in which I observed. The difference held in most of the cultures in which we did fieldwork together [including New England] . . . our access to data was different in every culture we studied, and although our interests and personalities may have contributed to some of these differences, our sex roles were also a most important element.

In sociology, contemporary concern with text has been not with field notes (which are rarely shared or used by others), but with the ways in which analysis and writing are affected by rhetorical devices (Gusfield, 1976), audiences (Stoddart, 1986; Warren, 1979), interviewee-interviewer gender (DeVault, 1986), and writing technique (Becker, 1985). Although anthropologists such as Wolf (1986) and Johnson (1986) have provided published accounts of rethinking one's inter-pretations of the field in the face of biographical alternations related to sexuality, gender, or feminism, in sociology such discussions have thus far remained within the domain of "corridor talk" (Rabinow, 1986).[18]

One of my own interests in recent years has been the use of gender frameworks in ethnography, in the context of historical and analytic changes within disciplines. My study of "schizophrenic women" and their husbands in the 1950s (1987) prompted me to rethink Goffman's (1961) and other 1950s-1970s ethnographies of mental hospital sick role and patienthood. These are essentially ungendered concepts, and ungendered texts. And yet we know that gender is visible to the observer; that Goffman, as he walked around the asylum, saw female and male mental patients. My analysis of the difference in gender focus between *Madwives* and *Asylums* is historical and methodological. First, Goffman was not, as I am, writing during a historical era where both theories and their discourses were the subject of feminist analysis. Second, the ethnographic and the intensive interview method reveal different aspects of the experience of being a mental patient. In brief, the ethnographic method focuses the observer's attention on staff-patient interaction, and the role of the mental patient. The rituals of the mental hospital, the stripping of identities, and the unfolding of the self-fulfilling prophecy are revealed by the ethnographer. The intensive interview, on the other hand, embeds the role of mental patient within the life course and historical self of the individual (Warren, 1987). And the salience of gender to the moral career of the 1950s female mental patient was made quite clear through the lens of the intensive interview *as the 1950s intensive interview was reread through the lens of 1980s social science* (see also DeVault, 1986).

Within anthropology, the most celebrated contemporary instance of ethnographic reinterpretation is the Mead-Freeman controversy over Mead's book *Coming of Age in Samoa* (1928). Taken not only as an ethnography of adolescence and sexual awakening among young girls in Samoa, but also as an indictment of child-rearing practices in the United States, Mead's book depicts an adolescence characterized by harmony rather than conflict. On the basis of his fieldwork in Samoa some fifteen years after Mead left, Derek Freeman (1983, pp. 240, 290) wrote in his book *Margaret Mead in Samoa: The Making and Unmaking of an Anthropological Myth* (1983) that Mead was "as a kind of joke, deliberately misled by her adolescent informants" with "counterfeit tales of casual love under the palm trees." Tiffany and Adams (1985, p. 27) contrast Mead's and Freeman's interpretations of Samoan adolescence:

> Whereas Mead found ease, cooperation and easy sex, Freeman found a pathology of conflict, violence and rape. Instead of a gentle upbringing within the secure warmth of an extended family, Freeman claimed that Samoan children are regularly subjected to harsh punishments by their parents. Instead of nurturance and sharing, Freeman found jealousy, competition and intense rivalry. Instead of adolescent boys and girls exploring the innocent pleasures of sex, Freeman described a society in which girls and women are terrorized by the omnipresent fear of brutal rape.

The fact that the Mead-Freeman debate is between a woman and a man have led other anthropologists to interpret these divergent accounts in a gendered context. First, the gender structure of Samoan society between Mead's and Freeman's visits perhaps provoked differential interpretation. Second, Freeman sought out, while Mead avoided, the male world of elite politics; Mead sought out, while Freeman avoided, the world of women and children (Tiffany & Adams, 1985). But the differences in their accounts of those occasions on which men and women come together, in sexual and family interactions, indicate that their entree into separate worlds of gender is not the only factor in their interpretive conflict. Tiffany and Adams (1985) suggest that Mead and Freeman were operating from within different anthropological allegories. Mead's text is infused with the pastoral or Edenic allegory of paradise lost (Clifford, 1986; Tiffany & Adams, 1985). Freeman, however, frames his in the dark allegory of the wild woman, "as powerless victim of savage lust. . . . Samoan women are depicted as brutalized sex objects, as well as violent aggressors" (Tiffany & Adams, 1985, p. 29):

> Samoan women are irrelevant in Freeman's analysis, except when they are duping Margaret Mead, punishing children, and fighting with other women over men. Samoan women are significant objects of scrutiny to Freeman the anthropologist when they are surreptitiously raped by "sleep-crawlers," or manually "deflowered" by chiefs in public ceremonies. Terrorized by their male assailants who are obsessed by the "cult of virginity" . . . and fantasies of forcible defloration and rape, Samoan women are transformed into debased Wild Women whose bodies provoke their own oppression.

Tiffany and Adams's reinterpretation of ethnographic reinterpretation reminds us of the hermeneutic circle that is ethnography. It also indicates that within the general allegories of the social science disciplines—the Western cultural "stories" within which other cultures are framed (Clifford, 1986)—there are often allegorical themes woven with the text of gender, and gender themes threaded through allegorical ones. We hear, for example, the voice of a disaffected male who finds a home in the gender-segregated world of the Abelam of Papua New Guinea (Scaglion, 1986). In a male-gendered version of the Edenic allegory, the male anthropologist depicts himself as finding a prefeminist paradise:

> I found Abelam sexual division of labor quite satisfying personally. . . . I have little interest in domestic tasks such as cooking and cleaning, performing them only grudgingly in the United States, so I was euphoric to be freed of them in the field. . . . I had no moral or ethical problems in assuming an air of sexual superiority consonant with that of the Abelam male. In fact, I am less comfortable with what are for me the redefined sex roles of men and women in the United States, for here I find myself trying to "watch" my sexism. (Scaglion, 1986, pp. 155-156)

Coming full circle, feminist discourse analysis itself is currently becoming the object of reinterpretation. Women social scientists sometimes find that feminist theories and assumptions are as problematic in understanding women's experience as are androcentric ones. In her analysis of her China notes, for example, Wolf (1986) found the feminist paradigm of the housebound woman-as-victim no more satisfying as an analytic tool than she had the androcentric model. Davis (1986, pp. 261-262) describes the "middle class, feminist, medical" bias that she brought to the study of the menopause experiences of Newfoundland women in the 1970s, saying:

> My biases were . . . sexist to the extent that I stereotyped the traditional female roles of mother and wife as simple and unsophisticated, chosen only by women because they lacked other opportunities or because they were afraid or incompetent to try anything else. I had entered the field believing that the best representatives of womanhood were those women most like myself, achievers in the public sphere.

The two volumes from which I draw some of the material in this monograph in themselves document the changes in the social science discourse of gender over the past twenty five years. The first is *Women in the Field: Anthropological Experiences*, edited by Peggy Golde, a collection of fourteen essays by women anthropologists first published in 1970 and republished in 1986. The second is *Self, Sex and Gender in Cross-Cultural Fieldwork,* edited by Tony Larry Whitehead and Mary Ellen Conaway, a collection of sixteen essays (six by men and ten by women), published in 1986. The 1986 edition of the Golde volume includes most of the original material unaltered, with the addition of a preface and a bibliography of later essays and books on sex and gender issues. The Whitehead and Conaway volume takes the Golde volume's generalizations about gender and sex in the field as a discussion point for the analysis made in their introduction and epilogue.

There are four major differences in the two volumes, differences that I think can be understood within the changing historical context of the social sciences. First, the Golde volume is about the experiences of women fieldworkers; as such, it reflects the first wave of feminist concern with the androcentrism of earlier fieldwork. By contrast, the later volume is by and about women and men in the field, reflecting not only a continuing concern with women's issues, but also a newer awareness of problems and processes in the field specific to men. Second, the Whitehead and Conaway volume utilizes specifically feminist theoretical perspectives in a way the Golde volume does not. Third, the Whitehead and Conaway volume makes more explicit references to the fieldworker's own sexual practices and interests than does the Golde volume, which refers to sexuality only in the language of illicit imputations on the one hand, and of licit marital offers on the other. And, finally, there are interesting, often subtle differences in conceptual and practical concerns in the two volumes; perhaps the most striking to me were the varying discussions of households and housework in the field, discussions that reflected the eras within which the research was conducted.

Most of the research projects described in the Golde volume took place in the late 1950s and early 1960s, although some were earlier (Landes, 1986). The accounts of households in the field indicate that women anthropologists in the 1950s and 1960s accepted relatively unproblematically the gender division of labor typical of that era in Western society: Essentially, that whatever the specifics, it was the woman who was "in charge" of the household. Although her husband was not working at the time of her fieldwork in Greece (the 1960s) and she was, Ernestine Friedl described her special problems as a "woman anthropologist *running* a household. . . . Had I had to do the housework under these primitive conditions, I would have had time for nothing else" (Friedl, 1986, p. 208, italics added). By contrast, writing about householding in the 1970s, Regina Oboler (1986, p. 39) noted that she and her husband "always divided domestic labor equally." Like the Friedl household, however, the Obolers conformed publicly to domestic gender roles during their fieldwork among the Nandi. Indeed, the Friedls in 1950s Greece and the Obolers in 1970s Kenya experienced many of the same problems not only of the public household division of labor, but of the assumption that it was the man who was in charge of the research enterprise (Friedl, 1986; Oboler, 1986).

Thus the analysis of ethnographic accountings must itself take into account changes in historical time. Generalizations made during one period of history may not obtain during another. The setting, research methods, disciplinary and personal biography of the fieldworker shape the process and productions of fieldwork; all this in turn is shaped by history. Analysis in the social sciences is an interpretive rather than a scientific process; one that takes place at the intersection of theory, method, discourse, and the historical moment. And gender is one of many themes within that intersection; as feminist theory, as discourse analysis, and as part of the historical self of both the observer and the observed. In all the activities of fieldwork, from the course of one's academic career, to entering the field, to putting on one's clothes in the morning, to writing up field notes and drafting articles for publication, gender shapes the task. It is inescapably so our task is to see the shaping through the shapes. But how do we do this?

4. WARNINGS AND ADVICE

The lack of connection between concepts of rapport and rhetoric, of anecdotes and analysis, is matched by a similar gap between the practical and the epistemological, the methods and the methodology. The methodological literature divides fairly evenly into sometimes abstruse philosophical discourses and practical recipes for action. I think that this great epistemological divide is in part a consequence of fieldwork mythology: the disciplinary tendency to classify experiences in the field according to models, stages, and taken-for-granted categories, such as "entree," "rapport," "research bargain," and "key informant." What, for example, is a not-key informant, and how do we know? These categories, in turn, are either stuffed with anecdotal instances (practical warnings and advice) or scrutinized for epistemological origins (the abstruse philosophy). In this section, I abandon epistemological scrutiny and focus on the pragmatic.

A standard overlapping-stage model of fieldwork is suggested by the methods literature: selecting a topic, the issue of team or "lone ranger" fieldwork, entree, developing relationships, trust, and rapport, writing field notes, beginning analysis, developing analysis, writing up findings, and leaving the field. At each of these stages the gender issues discussed in this volume are of considerable relevance; it is pragmatic, for example, for the novice anthropologist to find out something about the clothing and conduct deemed appropriate for women and men in the culture that will be his or her temporary home.

But it would also be useful, in the epistemological long run, to "bracket" the gender stories I have summarized above, and to see them as myths bound up with the discourse of fieldwork in the historically grounded "fields" of academia, rather than as mirrors of interactions in the field. Certain fundamental assumptions underlying social science fieldwork are, I think, gender biased. The 1920s-1960s language of objectivity in ethnography has given way to a discourse of "immersion and distance" (Emerson, 1983), but still the distance remains—the explicit or implicit instruction to the fieldworker not to get too close to informants. Mead (1986), the ultimate honorary male anthropologist, cautions against taking on the kind of fictive-kin roles experienced by Jean Briggs as "Kapluna daughter" on the grounds that such "simulated primary relationships draw too heavily on the fieldworker's own culture and distort and dim the observers' capacity to maintain that necessary distance that is both warm and limited, affectionate but not passionate, friendly but not partisan" (Mead, 1986, p. 324). As Evelyn Fox Keller (1985) notes, the persistent scientific call to objectivity, distance, and caution is quintessentially male.

Gender and Fieldwork Stages

The biographical experiences of women and men provoke varying responses to field sites and research topics. Deep emotional involvement in a setting or issue related to gender or sex can be motivating and productive of strong research interest; so much the methodological texts tell us (Lofland & Lofland, 1984). But there may also be issues or settings that arouse feelings of pain, such as Katz Rothman's work on amniocentesis. Fieldworkers cannot identify in detail the range and depth of feelings they will come to experience in the field. But some educated guesses can be made. I was asked recently to get involved in an ethnographic study of protective custody in women's prison. As in men's prison, protective custody is used mainly to keep women who have killed or battered their own children from being attacked by other inmates. As a new mother, I knew that I would not be able to approach such a setting without distress, so I declined the opportunity.

Since gender norms within the chosen setting shape the man's or woman's entree and research relationships, fieldworkers have to make decisions about the degree to which, and the ways in which, they will conform to local expectations. As Krieger (1986) notes, gender conformity and deviation in a given culture are processual, dialectical, and reflexive: They change over time, they are related to one another, and they affect not only relationships with respondents but also categories used in interpretation. She adds that gender role expectations in anthropological fieldwork consist of "at least four parts":

1. distinguishing between what informants are actually communicating about how they expect the anthropologist to behave and what preconceived ideas the anthropologist brings with her or him; 2. distinguishing between what informants expect of one another and what they expect of the anthropologist; 3. distinguishing between aspects of gender role that are crucial and cannot be broken, even by an educated foreigner, and 4.

determining how to break or bend gender expectations to gain the freedom necessary to collect data. (Krieger, 1986, p. 118)

Krieger cautions the anthropologist going to a new setting to be as prepared as possible with information about gender roles in the culture, but also to remain open to learning about permitted deviance: ways in which norms differ from behavior, or norms for foreigners differ from norms for natives. Both her four principles and her discussion of anticipatory and field socialization into gender norms are applicable not only to anthropology but also to sociology, although the norms themselves are not as problematic to sociologists familiar with their own culture. While a Western woman going to Burma has to be informed that wearing fresh flowers in her hair will be well received, a woman going to the local district attorney's office does not have to be told that this same body adornment will seem slightly strange to the legal natives. Anthropologists learn about gender norms in different cultures by talking to and reading the work of other anthropologists; sociologists learn through their own socialization and status as cultural insiders.

Conforming to local gender norms may take personal changes that some social scientists are more, and others are less, willing to consider. In her discussion of fieldwork in Guatemala, for example, Nancie Gonzalez discusses the problems associated with being a female head of household, and a divorced woman. In this Roman Catholic environment, it was her divorced status that eventually posed the most difficulties (Gonzalez, 1986, p. 92). Gonzalez notes that if she had to plan the research over again she would "invent widowhood with appropriate rings and photographs" in order to avoid the stigma of divorce. Other social scientists would not be prepared to alter their autobiographies in this manner. Similarly, some anthropological couples are willing to compromise such features of their everyday life as household labor equality in the field site while others are not (compare, for example, Oboler [1986] and Fleuhr-Lobban & Lobban [1986]).

For the practicalities of gender are related not only to "lone gun" but also to team field research, especially in anthropology. The fieldwork accounts of husband-wife and other cross-gender teams in the field indicate both advantages and disadvantages of collaboration. As noted above, husband-wife teamwork in the field give the researcher unique insights into worlds separated by gender (Fleuhr-Lobban & Lobban, 1986; Friedl, 1986; Golde, 1986; Oboler, 1986). On the other hand, the management of a household, especially if it includes children, can be a burden on the research process, both in the amount of time it takes away from fieldwork, and in the refuge it provides from having to make socioemotional connections with informants (Whitehead & Price, 1986). Disadvantages include the strain on a marital relationship that comes with the terrain of fieldwork (Whitehead & Price, 1986), and the "unique access" afforded the single female researcher by the "tendency of people in many cultures to want to adopt" them (Whitehead & Price, 1986, p. 299).

In the few sociological commentaries on team field research, the gender division of labor is taken for granted, as is differential access to meanings by gender (Douglas, 1975; Warren & Rasmussen, 1979). This is perhaps because in sociology the typical research setting is temporally limited; the fieldworker can go back to his or her spouse at night, take research partners of different genders into the field, or go it alone, as circumstances dictate. The sociologist is not usually assigned a place within the local kinship network. But at least one published account indicates that, for sociologists as well as anthropologists, marriage and other social relationships can become competing commitments to the research endeavor. In the context of changing domestic gender norms in our society—at least among academics—an all-male fieldworker team in the 1980s can no longer rely on housewives to take care of domestic routines while they do research. One researcher commented:

> Being married and having family responsibilities, I find usually that I have to go home and attend to those responsibilities. That means that I have difficulty getting notes down quickly, so there's a time lag . . . between the time of my observations and the time I am able to dictate them. . . . I had to come home and be a father to my child and a husband to my wife, and then babysit[19] while my wife went back to work. This certainly interferes with trying to get verbatim quotes down. On the other hand, I am not prepared to sacrifice my family life any more than I already have. (Shaffir et al., 1980, p. 60)

Choices must be made not only of what research to engage in but also what to include or omit in writing up research reports. Issues of gender and sex, as indicated above, have been dealt with to varying degrees and in varying ways depending upon the disciplinary biases in vogue at the moment. From the 1920s until very recently, for example, fieldworkers were not encouraged to be self-reflexive in their published accounts, avoiding the discussion of emotions in the service of objectivity and the elimination of bias. The topic of sexuality was particularly taboo.

Today, methodological treatises encourage the reporting not only of emotions but of sexual involvements in the field (Whitehead & Price, 1986). Yet it is not always clear why sexual encounters should be reported, beyond a modern "confessional" impulse. It seems to me that where sexual expectations and encounters are part of the public discourse, and where the researcher's participation is analytically salient—for example, in Turnbull's and Styles's research—then there is good reason to write about it. Where the discussion of sexuality illuminates little more than the researcher's personal odysseys—then I think that it becomes gratuitous. And there are contexts in which the public discussion of sexuality can be damaging to a career in academia; for example, the publicizing of homosexual preference or gay identity through methodological fieldwork accounts. Although there is a public norm of tolerance among social scientists, this may not extend to other disciplines whose university members sit in judgment on such matters as tenure. And the public norm of tolerance is just that: public. Listening to decades of gossip among colleagues has convinced me that whatever it may do for an individual's sense of self, publicly coming "out of the closet" rarely does much for their careers.

Although sexuality is currently "coming out of the closets" and into the texts, some aspects of the body remain within the domain of what Rabinow (1986) calls "corridor talk," or the communicative-socializing talk that occurs between colleagues and graduate students. There may be a gender direction in what constitutes published and what constitutes corridor domains; one example that comes to mind is menstruation. Although there are numerous published substantive accounts of menstrual taboos in non-Western cultures, I could find no meth-odological accounts of how female researchers deal with their own menstruation in such societies.[20] Anecdotes from corridor talk include the dilemma of a female anthropologist who was planning to be carried up a mountain on a litter at the time when her period was starting. If she told the men who were to carry her litter about her period, they would no longer agree to do so. If she did not do so, she would be in radical violation of local gender norms. She ended up not telling the men, and hoping that they did not find out.

Gender Mythology in Fieldwork Texts

Despite the current focus on textual revelation, I think there is a place for corridor talk within fieldwork's oral traditions; not everything needs to be textual. Whether published or anecdotal, however, the methodological tales told by fieldworkers should be understood not simply as recipes for action, or as warnings and advice, but also as a rich folkloric tradition in their own right. I will give some examples of current gender folklore, and indicate the ways in which fieldworkers might become more sensitive to counterinstances that challenge existing accounts.

The focal gender myth of field research is the greater communicative skills and less threatening nature of the female fieldworker. I think it is important for both novice and experienced fieldworkers to approach this and other myths not as revealed truths about fieldwork relations, but as accounts—as texts in their own right, to be read as texts. We know, for example, that fieldworkers in other historical contexts have reversed the gender myth (Cressey, 1983). So we might ask another question, as fieldworkers: What do the field note and ethnographic accounts of women's sensitivity in the field tell us about the place of women in our own Western, academic "field," about the sort of work they do, and ways they are seen? Similarly, what does the fact of a quite different emphasis by gender tell us about our own culture's sexual scripts? Female and male fieldworkers who are aware of the mythology of gender issues should try to become aware of counterexamples from their own fieldwork experiences. For example, in *The Court of Last Resort* (1982) I wrote about sexual hustling by males in the court, rather than about my having flirted, or pursued the available men. I tried to think back over the research experience to determine whether or not I engaged in behavior that could be fit to the male researcher paradigm; unfortunately it was too long ago, and I did not remember much. But I can recall (because it took place over a few weeks) a series of incidents where I first tried to find out about the marital status of and then gently pursued one of the attorneys (by making sure I ran into him, stretching my research agenda in that direction). It would not have occurred to me even to write these incidents down in my field notes, let alone in the published Appendix. It was not that I was ashamed or afraid, it was simply that I never thought of it: The gender/methods literature pointed in the direction of reporting sexual hustling of female researchers by male informants, not the other way around. Researchers can also bring into conscious awareness the circumstances under which their methodological accounts are "laundered," either to protect "oppressed" respondents or the researcher's appearance of professional competence (Gurney, 1983), both of which could differ by gender. Warnings and advice, in the last analysis, are pale echoes of fieldwork realities, general principles abstracted from the thick context of research done at other times in other places, by other men and women. Entering the field, developing a place within the social order, talking, feeling, and living in the setting, are the terrain of understanding the intersection of gender, self, and others in fieldwork. Writing field notes, writing essays, seeking and incorporating reviews and editing, are the terrain of understanding the web of data, self, and discourse. The final warning and advice, I think, must be: Go into the field, and live, and think, and write. Listen to what we others have said, but do not let our voices become too much the shapers of yours. It is not "any researcher" who produces a particular ethnography, it is you.

NOTES

1. Grateful thanks to John Van Maanen, Bob Emerson, Nancy Lutkehaus, Bill Staples, Clifford Staples, Barrie Thorne, Constance Ahrons, Peter Manning, and John Johnson for comments on earlier drafts.

2. I suspect that anthropologists have been more attuned to gender issues in fieldwork than sociologists, at least from the 1920s to the mid-1970s, because gender norms in non-Western cultures are mysterious rather than taken-for-granted as the social scientist's own.

3. Because I am unable, in this short volume, to consider the question of age in any detail, I have omitted a discussion of the ethnography of age and gender in education as represented by sociologists such as Barrie Thorne in the United States and Paul Willis in England.

4. Like many aging fieldworkers, I have retreated of late to historical and interview research.

5. These sections are presented quite disparately; furthermore, the monograph has no concluding section in which the themes I trace are tied neatly together. It is part of the nature of the fieldwork literature, I think, that discussions of practical and epistemological issues, and of research relationships and analysis, tend to be unconnected. It is beyond the scope of my discussion here to attempt a grand synthesis. And I suspect that such a synthesis may not be possible; gender, like other concepts, may be framed in a variety of different ways.

6. There are several excellent histories of the Chicago school, including Jim Thomas's excellent special issue of *Urban Life* (1983). None of them, however, takes a gendered perspective on the 1920s-1930s Chicago experience.

7. See Warren (1984) for a critique of the concepts (or "myths") of trust and rapport in fieldwork.

8. Again, these are the personal characteristics seen as significant in Western culture. It may be that another culture sees as highly significant the length of toes, but the fieldworker might not even discover the other's close—if covert—observation of her or his feet.

9. Achieving a status such as honorary male, and access to men's rituals and ceremonies, may be facilitated as readily—more readily perhaps—by paying informants in money or goods as by the persevering development of trust and rapport. This principle may be true of numerous sorts of anthropological transactions.

10. It is part of the folklore of contemporary sociology that there is an advantage to both fieldwork and interviewing in minority communities if the researcher is of the same racial and ethnic background as those he or she is studying. This "matching" theory of rapport is also illustrated by the injunction that women should study women, young people the young, and so on.

11. One exception is if the males in question are gay and so are the bars. I was able to do "drinking" research in the gay male community with little risk of sexual overtures, although they did occasionally occur.

12. I speak here of sexual behavior itself as having no ritual place; reputed sexual involvements (real or imagined) have a highly ritualized place in organizational gossip. And gossip, in turn, is consequential for the conduct of organizational life. Interestingly, Kanter's (1977) book on corporate life, one of the few ethnographies that deals with corporate executives, wives, and secretaries, barely touches on questions of sexual gossip.

13. I have learned much about fieldwork methods from the many graduate students in sociology (and more recently also anthropology) at the University of Southern California who have written ethnographies under my supervision. Liz Brunner is one of them.

14. I was going to delete the phrase "in my own academic life" as redundant, but then hesitated to do so. I realized that my unwillingness to delete the phrase was a function of my desire not to be seen as totally out of date in the realm of sexual politics (see Hunt's [1984] critique of my [1977] admission of sexist responses and hiring practices).

15. This summary is taken from comments made by anthropologist colleagues that they did not wish attributed to them.

16. It may be that the older the cohort of academic women, the more likely the history of drift. I came to this conclusion from conversations with older (for example, Matilda White Riley in sociology) and younger (for example, Nancy Lutkehaus in anthropology) cohorts.

17. Examples of this approach include Clifford and Marcus (1985; anthropology); Gusfield (1976; sociology), Stoddart (1986; sociology); and Nicholson, (1986; history).

18. In talks he routinely gives, for example, Laud Humphreys, the author of *Tearoom Trade* now openly acknowledges his homosexuality, and his sexual participation in the tearooms. But he has also undergone a significant biographical change: As a committed member of a self-help group, he sees himself as an alcoholic, an "addictive personality," whose tearoom behavior reflected compulsion rather than choice. When asked how he would rewrite *Tearoom Trade* today he replied that he would frame the interpretation through the concept of the addictive personality, and take note of the fact that the tearoom participants he studied were acting compulsively, and were mostly alcoholics.

19. Despite the language of child-care and housework equality in modern professional households, a less egalitarian language reflects a more traditional division of labor. A mother would not describe child care as "babysitting," the language of outsiders.

20. Indeed, although there is much discussion of the symbolic aspects of menstrual taboos, there is little written about the practicalities of menstruation: how a monthly flow is handled in societies without tampons or laundromats. I suspect that this way of framing the issue of menstruation (as so many other issues) is a consequence of the androcentric dominance of males in ethnographic theory.

REFERENCES

Agar, M. H. (1986). *Speaking of ethnography*. Newbury Park, CA: Sage.

Angrosino, M. V. (1986). "Son and lover: The anthropologist as non-threatening male." In T. L. Whitehead & M. E. Conaway (Eds.), *Self, sex and gender in cross-cultural fieldwork* (pp. 64-83). Urbana: University of Illinois Press.

Barham, P. (1984). *Schizophrena and human value*. New York: Basil Blackwell.

Becker, H. S. (1986). *Writing for social scientists: How to start and finish your thesis, book or article*. Chicago: University of Chicago Press.

Briggs, J. (1986). "Kapluna daughter." In P. Golde (Ed.), *Women in the field: Anthropological experiences* (2nd ed., pp. 19-44). Berkeley: University of California Press.

Bulmer, M. (1983, April). "The methodology of the taxi dance hall: An early account of Chicago ethnography from the 1920s." *Urban Life, 12*, 95-101.

Clifford, J. (1986). "On ethnographic allegory." In J. Clifford & G. E. Marcus (Eds.), *Writing culture: The poetics and politics of ethnography* (pp. 98-121). Berkeley: University of California Press.

Codere, H. (1986). "Field Work in Rwanda, (1959-1960)." In P. Golde (Ed.), *Women in the field: Anthropological experiences* (pp. 143-164). Berkeley: University of California Press.

Conaway, M. E. (1986). "The pretense of the neutral researcher." In T. L. Whitehead & M. E. Conaway (Eds.), *Self, sex and gender in cross-cultural fieldwork* (pp. 52-63). Urbana: University of Illinois Press.

Cressey, P. G. (1986, April). "Comparison of the roles of the 'sociological stranger' and the 'anonymous stranger' in field research." *Urban Life, 12*, 102-120.

Davis, D. (1986). "Changing self-image: Studying menopausal women in a Newfoundland fishing village." In T. L. Whitehead & M. E. Conaway (Eds.), *Self, sex and gender in cross-cultural fieldwork* (pp. 240-261). Urbana: University of Illinois Press.

DeVault, M. L. (1986, August). *Talking and listening from women's standpoints: Feminist strategies for analyzing interview data*. Paper presented at the annual meetings of the Society for the Study of Symbolic Interaction, New York.

Douglas, J. D. (1979). *Investigative social research: Individual and team field research*. Newbury Park, CA: Sage.

Douglas, J. D. (1985). *Creative interviewing*. Newbury Park, CA: Sage.

Douglas, J. D., P. Rasmussen, & C. A. Flanagan. (1977). *The nude beach*. Newbury Park, CA: Sage.

Easterday, L., D. Papademas, L. Schorr, & C. Valentine. (1977, October). "The making of a female researcher: Role problems in field work." *Urban Life, 6*, 333-348.

Faithorn, E. (1986). "Gender bias and sex bias: Removing our cultural blinders in the field." In T. L. Whitehead & M. E. Conaway (Eds.), *Self, sex and gender in cross-cultural fieldwork* (pp. 275-288). Urbana: University of California Press.

Ferraro, K. J. (1983, October). "Negotiating trouble in a battered women's shelter." *Urban Life, 12,* 287-306

Fischer, A. (1986). "Field work in five cultures." In P. Golde (Ed.), *Women in the field: Anthropological experiences* (pp. 267-289). Berkeley: University of California Press.

Fleuhr-Lobban, C., & R. A. Lobban. (1986). "Families, gender and methodology in the Sudan." In T. L. Whitehead & M. E. Conaway (Eds.), *Self, sex and Gender in cross-cultural fieldwork* (pp. 152-195). Urbana: University of Illinois Press.

Foucault, M. (1978). *The history of sexuality: Introduction.* New York: Pantheon.

Foucault, M. (1980). *Power/knowledge.* New York: Pantheon.

Freeman, D. (1983). *Margaret Mead in Samoa: The making and unmaking of an anthropological myth.* Cambridge: MA: Harvard University Press.

Freedman, D. (1986). "Wife, widow, woman: Roles of an anthropologist in a Transylvanian village." In P. Golde (Ed.), *Women in the field: Anthropological experiences* (pp. 335-358). Berkeley: University of California Press.

Friedl, E. (1980). "Field work in a Greek village." In P. Golde (Ed.), *Women in the field: Anthropological experiences* (pp. 195-236). Berkeley: University of California Press.

Fuller, L. (forthcoming). "Field work in forbidden terrain." *American Sociologist.*

Golde, P. (1986). "Odyssey of encounter." In P. Golde (Ed.), *Women in the field: Anthropological experiences* (pp. 67-93). Berkeley: University of California Press.

Gonzalez, N. (1986). "The anthropologist as female head of household." In T. L. Whitehead & M. E. Conaway (Eds.), *Self, sex and gender in cross-cultural fieldwork* (pp. 84-100). Urbana: University of Illinois Press.

Gurney, J. N. (1985, Spring). "Not one of the guys: The female researcher in a male-dominated setting." *Qualitative Sociology, 8,* 42-62.

Gusfield, J. (1976). "The literary rhetoric of science: Comedy and pathos in drinking driver research." *American Sociological Review, 41,* 16-34.

Hochschild, A. R. (1983). *The managed heart: Commercialization of human feeling.* Berkeley: University of California Press.

Humphreys, L. (1979). *Tearoom trade: Impersonal sex in public places* (enlarged ed.). Chicago: Aldine.

Hunt, J. (1984). "The development of rapport through the negotiation of gender in field work among police." *Human Organization, 43,* 283-296.

Jackson, J. (1986). "On trying to be an Amazon." In T. L. Whitehead & M. E. Conaway (Eds.), *Self, sex and gender in cross-cultural fieldwork* (pp. 263-274). Urbana: University of Illinois Press.

Johnson, J. M. (1975). *Doing field research.* London: Free Press.

Johnson, N. B. (1986). "Ethnographic research and rites of incorporation: A sex- and gender-based comparison." In T. L. Whitehead & M. E. Conaway (Eds.), *Self, sex and gender in cross-cultural fieldwork* (pp. 164-181). Urbana: University of Illinois Press.

Kanter, R. B. (1977). *Men and women of the corporation.* New York: Basic Books.

Katz, B. R. (1986). "Reflections: On hard work." *Qualitative Sociology, 9,* 48-53.

Keller, E. F. (1985). *Reflections on gender and science.* Yale: Yale University Press.

Krieger, L. (1986). "Negotiating gender role expectations in Cairo." In T. L. Whitehead & M. E. Conaway (Eds.), *Self, sex and gender in cross-cultural fieldwork* (pp. 117-128). Urbana: University of Illinois Press.

Kuper, A. (1973). *Anthropologists and anthropology: The British school, 1922-1972.* New York: Pica.

70

Landes, R. (1986). "A woman anthropologist in Brazil." In P. Golde (Ed.), *Women in the field: Anthropological experiences* (pp. 119-139). Berkeley: University of California Press.

Lederman, R. (1986). "The Return of redwoman: Field work in highland New Guinea." In P. Golde (Ed.), *Women in the field: Anthropological experiences* (pp. 361-388). Berkeley: University of California Press.

Lofland, J., & L. Lofland. (1985). *Analyzing social settings: A guide to qualitative observations and research.* Belmont, CA: Wadsworth.

Lutkehaus, N. (1982, December). "Ambivalence, ambiguity and the reproduction of gender hierarchy in Manam society, 1933-1979." *Social Analysis, 12*, 36-93.

Lutkehaus, N. (forthcoming a). "Reflections of reality: On the use of other ethnographers' fieldnotes." In R. Sanjek (Ed.), *Fieldnotes.* Unpublished manuscript.

Lutkehaus, N. (forthcoming b). "She was *very* Cambridge: Camilla Wedgwood and the history of women in British social anthropology." *American Ethnologist, 13.*

Mead, M. (1923). *Coming of age in Samoa.* New York: William Morrow.

Mead, M. (1986). "Field work in Pacific islands, 1925-1967." In P. Golde (Ed.), *Women in the field: Anthropological experiences* (pp. 293-331). Berkeley: University of California Press.

Nader, L. (1986). "From anguish to exultation." In P. Golde (Ed.), *Women in the field: Anthropological experiences* (pp. 97-116). Berkeley: University of California Press.

Nicholson, L. J. (1986). *Gender and history: The limits of social theory in the age of the family.* New York: Columbia University Press.

Oboler, R. S. "For Better or worse: Anthropologists and husbands in the field." In T. L. Whitehead & M.E. Conaway (Eds.), *Self, sex and gender in cross-cultural fieldwork* (pp. 28-51). Urbana: University of Illinois Press.

Palmer, V. M. (1928). *Field studies in sociology: A student's manual.* Chicago: University of Chicago Press.

Rabinow, P. (1986). "Representations are social facts." In J. Clifford & G. E. Marcus (Eds.), *Writing culture: The poetics and politics of ethnography* (pp. 234-261). Berkeley: University of California Press.

Rovner-Piecznik, R. (1976). "Another kind of education: Researching urban justice." In M. P. Golden (Ed.), *The research experience* (pp. 465-473). Itasca, IL: F. E. Peacock.

Rubin, L. (1976). *Worlds of pain: Life in the working-class family.* New York: Basic Books.

Sass, L. (1986, May). "Anthropology's native problems: Revisionism in the field." *Harpers Magazine,* pp. 49-57.

Scaglion, R. (1986). "Sexual segregation and ritual pollution in Abelam society." In T. L. Whitehead & M. E. Conaway (Eds.), *Self, sex and gender in cross-cultural fieldwork* (pp. 151-163). Urbana: University of Illinois Press.

Shaffir, W., V. Marshall, & J. Haas. (1980, January). "Competing commitments: Unanticipated problems of field research." *Qualitative Sociology, 2*, 56-71.

Shostak, M. (1981). *Nisa: The life and words of a !Kung woman.* Cambridge, MA: Harvard University Press.

Smith, R. J. (1986). "Hearing voices, joining the chorus: Appropriating someone else's fieldnotes." In R. Sanjek (Ed.), *Fieldnotes.* Unpublished manuscript.

Stoddart, K. (1986). "The presentation of everyday life: Some textual strategies for 'adequate ethnography.'" *Urban Life, 15*, 103-121.

Strathern, M. (1984, July 4). "Dislodging a world view: Challenge and counter-challenge in the relationship between feminism and anthropology." Paper presented at the Research Center for Women's Studies, University of Adelaide.

Styles, J. (1979, July). "Outsider/insider: Researching gay baths." *Urban Life, 2*, 235-252.

Sudarkasa, N. (1986). "In a world of women: Field work in a Yoruba community." In P. Golde (Ed.), *Women in the field: Anthropological experiences* (pp. 167-191). Berkeley: University of California Press.

Thompson, K. (1986). "Exploring American Indian communities in depth." In P. Golde (Ed.), *Women in the field: Anthropological experiences* (pp. 47-64). Berkeley: University of California Press.

Tiffany, S. W., & K. J. Adams. (1985). *The wild woman: An inquiry into the anthropology of an idea.* Cambridge, MA: Schenkman.

Turnbull, C. M. (1986). "Sex and gender: The role of subjectivity in field research." In T. L. Whitehead & M. E. Conaway (Eds.), *Self, sex and gender in cross-cultural fieldwork* (pp. 17-27). Urbana: University of Illinois Press.

Warren, C.A.B. (1972). *Identity and community in the gay world.* New York: Wiley-Interscience.

Warren, C.A.B. (1982). *The court of last resort: Mental illness and the law.* Chicago: University of Chicago Press.

Warren, C.A.B. (1984). "Toward a captive model of qualitative research." *Communication Quarterly, 2*, 104-112.

Warren, C.A.B. (1987). *Madwives: Schizophrenic women in the 1950s.* Rutgers, NJ: Rutgers University Press.

Warren, C.A.B., & P. K. Rasmussen. (1977, October). "Sex and gender in fieldwork research." *Urban Life, 6*, 359-369.

Wax, R. H. (1979, June). "Gender and age in fieldwork and fieldwork education: No good thing is done by any man alone." *Social Problems, 26*, 509-522.

Wedgwood, C. (1957). "The education of women and girls in the Pacific." *South Pacific, 9*, 495-501.

Weidman, H. H. (1986). "On ambivalence in the field." In P. Golde (Ed.), *Women in the field: Anthropological experiences* (pp. 239-263). Berkeley: University of California Press.

Whitehead, T. L. (1986). "Breakdown, resolution and coherence: The fieldwork experiences of a big, brown pretty-talking man in a West Indian Community." In T. L. Whitehead & M. E. Conaway (Eds.), *Self, sex and gender in cross-cultural fieldwork* (pp. 213-239). Urbana: University of Illinois Press.

Whitehead, T. L., & M. E. Conaway (1986). "Introduction." In T. L. Whitehead & M. E. Conaway (Eds.), *Self, sex and gender in cross-cultural fieldwork* (pp. 1-14). Urbana: University of Illinois Press.

Whitehead, T. L., & L. Price. (1986). "Summary: Sex and the fieldwork experience." In T. L. Whitehead & M. E. Conaway (Eds.), *Self, sex and gender in cross-cultural fieldwork* (pp. 305-308). Urbana: University of Illinois Press.

Wolf, M. (1986). "Chinanotes: Engendering anthropology." In R. Sanjek (Ed.), *Fieldnotes.* Unpublished manuscript.

ABOUT THE AUTHOR

CAROL A.B. WARREN is a Professor of Sociology in the Department of Sociology and Social Science Research Institute of the University of Southern California. Her research interests include fieldwork methodology, gender and age in relation to the history of psychiatric treatment, and discourse analysis. She is the author of *The Court of Last Resort: Mental Illness and the Law* (1982, University of Chicago Press) and *Madwives: Schizophrenic Women in the 1950s* (1987, Rutgers University Press).